More Memories
of
Liverpool

Part of the
Memories
series

*The Publishers would like to thank the following companies for supporting
the production of this book*

Main Sponsor

Smith & Bateson

Bahr Behrend & Co. Limited

Griffiths & Armour

Harrison Line

T J Hughes

Edmund Kirby

Lawtons Limited

Liverpool School of Tropical Medicine

Marconi Communications

Mersey Travel

MPE Limited

Nelsons of Aintree

The Nugent Care Society

Porter Bros Limited

Rathbones

Rewinds & J Windsor & Sons (Engineers) Limited

Royal & SunAlliance

First published in Great Britain by True North Books Limited
Units 3 - 5 Heathfield Industrial Park
Elland West Yorkshire
HX5 9AE
Tel. 01422 377977
© Copyright: True North Books Limited 2000

ISBN 1 903204 09 7

Printed and bound by Butler & Tanner Ltd, Frome and London

Liverpool through the years

Nothing ever stays the same, and we cannot progress without change. Some changes, however, hurt more than others - as did those the Luftwaffe carried out during the second world war, when they left the docks, the suburbs, and much of Liverpool's main shopping area in smouldering ruins. The planners were not far behind the German planes, and many more of our buildings were to be sacrificed as Liverpool fell and rose again, like the fabled phoenix, from the ashes - though in a vastly changed form.

The city's new architecture was stark and angular, and as the 1950s progressed to the 60s many were to react against the characterless 'square box' buildings that were replacing the old shops, banks, pubs and churches - many of which had been architectural gems. But, as is always the case, we learned to live with the 'new' city, and parts of it we learned to love.

We are fortunate that the 20th century was so well chronicled, and this collection of fascinating images calls to mind the city as it was in our youth - and long before that! We visit vanished cinemas such as the Forum and the Palais de Luxe, take a peek at Blackler's and Bunneys, and experience the adrenalin rush of the Grand National.

This new collection reproduces these and many more nostalgic images to remind us of the way we once lived. We hope that you will read and enjoy 'More Memories of Liverpool' - and remember that history is still in the making.

Contents

The streets of change

The 'Penny in the Pound fund' (now called Medi-Cash) was a scheme to help pay towards medical costs. Perhaps some of our readers will remember participating in this scheme, which was run by the Merseyside Hospitals Council. As interesting as the buildings of bygone Liverpool are the glimpses of past fashions. Hemlines, as we know, rise and fall over the years according to the latest fads. When this view was captured in the late 1940s the fashions of wartime Britain were still in vogue; a few years on the young ladies passing the windows of British Home Stores would not be showing nearly so much leg! Mid calf length, widely flared skirts were to become the 'in thing' during the 1950s. Remember paper-nylon under-skirts? And those frothy net ones? Lady readers who were in their teens and twenties during the '50s certainly will. Immensely feminine, the crisp petticoats transformed a loosely hanging skirt into a mini 'crinoline' that rustled seductively as they walked. And perhaps our male readers will remember with nostalgia those occasional tanta-lising glimpses of foaming petticoat!

This photograph, dating from 1947, will surely take our more mature readers on a trip down Memory Lane - or, to be more precise, Lord Street. Buses and cars are a thing of the past of course today, and though BHS remains, Mothercare, and more recently Gap, took the place of Hope Brothers, one of Liverpool's many well-respected tailors, where many of our readers will have ordered a new suit in days gone by. The Times Furnishing Company, you may remember, was a favourite place for window shopping. After dark, when all the shops were closed and the windows were

ablaze with light, young men and women planning to put together their first home, and married couples with young families, would make a beeline for this store. Even the children were charmed by the layout of the complete rooms in the windows, where modern three-piece suites and shiny walnut

sideboards and dining room suites could be admired and pictured within a home setting. Hire purchase agreements meant that the old 'utility' furniture could at last be sold, scrapped, or put away out of sight, and as the 1950s began, so did a whole new life for the new generation of young married people.

It's a long time since the rattle of trams was heard in Church Street, and we had to beware of oncoming traffic! Church Street was eventually to become a pedestrianised area, and though some of us might miss the old town, parents pushing buggies and with young children in tow are especially grateful for the safety of the traffic free streets. The sun shone brightly on Liverpool the day a photographer recorded this nostalgic scene for us around 70 years ago, and white blinds were lowered to protect the shop windows on the sunny side of the street. The sight of the old trams gives us a lot of pleasure today, and most Scousers will already know that Merseyside had the very first trams in Britain - drawn by horses, of course, before the advent of electricity. The system was set up by the appropriately named George Francis Train in Birkenhead in 1860. With the ability to carry 48 passengers upstairs and down, the new railed transport had nearly double the capacity of the old horse buses. By the 1870s most towns had trams, and by the end of the decade Britain had more than 200 miles of tramway.

an automatic signalling system, and the first to use all electric signals with coloured lights. A truly amazing feat of engineering which set Liverpool apart as a city which was not afraid to lead the way in utilising every modern development.

Top: 'Thank you very much for the Aintree iron' sang the Scaffold back in the 1960s. Over the 170 years since the foundation stone was laid in the first new grandstand, many have given thanks for the Aintree iron - though many more have not! A long line of trams has brought the punters to try their luck on Race Day in this marvellous 1920s photograph; no shadow then of today's huge free car park and its park and ride operation! Those were the days when the morning of the Grand National saw the adrenalin begin to flow and enormous crowds descend on the city, many of them from the overnight boat from Dublin. The advent in the 1950s of television cameras mounted on vehicles which kept up with the horses meant that people could see as much and more from their own fireside than they could by attending the event, and inevitably the numbers of people in the stands decreased. The nostalgia of the old days, however, still remains. How many readers descended on Aintree and walked the course on 'Jump Sunday', the Sunday before the race? Remember the air of excitement and anticipation? Those were the days! Jump Sunday was discontinued in the late 50s - the mess people left behind them meant a costly clearing up operation.

Above: The last train had already run on the 'Dockers' Umbrella', and this view - taken in 1957 - would soon change for ever as the workers moved in to dismantle the structure. Why did this marvellous stretch of railway have to go? Admittedly, by the 1950s the structure had deteriorated and was badly in need of renovation, but surely funding could have been found and this important part of Liverpool's heritage saved from the scrap merchant? So many 'firsts' were connected with the overhead railway, which was a real innovation when it was opened back in 1893. It was the first electric elevated railway in the world and the only elevated railway in the whole of Britain. It was the first railway to have

Both pictures: From our viewpoint looking across the Old Haymarket back in 1934, we can see that the area above street level was a network of tram wires. Those were the days before virtually every family owned a car, and public transport was the accepted way to get around the city, whether you were travelling to and from work or going to a dance or a city centre cinema. So much has changed since this photograph was taken, though the Blackburn Assurance Company's building still survives *(inset)*. The date 1934 neatly pinpoints the year the Mersey Tunnel opened, and the huge pillar which once stood near the entrance is under construction, surrounded by scaffolding. The building of the tunnel was obviously a magnet for interested passers-by - no matter what kind of work is in progress, the sight of men working has always attracted people to watch them. Dig a hole anywhere, and people will gather to gaze into it! We can assume, though, that the humble flat cap would have been the hardest hat on site during the construction of the tunnel. 'No hat, no

boots, no job' is the slogan that reflects today's emphasis on workers' safety, but 70 years or so ago employees undertook many dangerous jobs every day without gauntlets, safety glasses, hard hats or protective clothing of any kind, and reflected very little on the risk factor. Work on the tunnel had begun in 1925, and 3rd of April 1928 was a red letter day in the process of construction. The Liverpool side of the newly dug tunnel met up with the Birkenhead side - and after month after month of work that called for something special in the way of cele-

bration. In a novel ceremony to mark the occasion, the Lord Mayor of Liverpool, Miss Margaret Beavan, formally shook hands with Alderman Alec Naylor, the Mayor of Birkenhead, through a hole in the excavations. King George V officially opened the Queensway Tunnel in 1934, and Liverpool was well and truly linked to Birkenhead and the Wirral. The tunnel, which cost a total of £7.75 million, descends a 1 in 30 gradient before levelling off below the river, and rising again through the same gradient to Birkenhead.

Both pictures: As long ago as the early 19th century there was a recognised need for a tunnel beneath the Mersey, and the original plans were for a two-tier tunnel with public transport below (at the time, trams) and motor cars on top. During the early part of the 20th century, the planners favoured the idea of a bridge. There were many drawbacks to the plan, however, not least that of the shipping on the Mersey, and with the start of the second world war the idea was shelved and eventually disappeared into oblivion.

Work on the tunnel began in 1925, and at 2.13 miles long the Mersey Tunnel was the longest underwater road tunnel in the world when it was completed in 1934. Liverpool City Council solved the problem of what to do with the rock and debris from the excavations, arousing worldwide interest by using it to develop a riverside promenade and park at Otterspool, which was opened to the public in 1950.

The opening of the tunnel had a devastating effect on the ferries, of course, and in fact the full impact on the goods ferry was vastly underestimated. The tunnel officially opened on 18th July, and by October ferry revenue had fallen from around £2,500 to £260 a week. Many of the ferries' staff were transferred to tunnel duties.

As traffic levels increased over the years the road bridge idea surfaced once more, and plans for building a six-lane bridge across the river were put forward, only to be rejected by the Cheshire authorities. Instead, a second Mersey tunnel, Kingsway, was built between Liverpool and Wallasey. The Kingsway Tunnel was opened by the Queen in 1971, and a further tunnel was in use by the mid 1970s. Since that time a one-way traffic system has been devised for Liverpool and flyovers constructed, and new approach roads have been laid down in Birkenhead. The city's traffic now flows more smoothly, and changes and improvements are ongoing.

Above: Isn't it amazing how familiarity can breed, if not contempt, at least inattention? Passers-by in Islington appear to be so used to seeing Liverpool's splendid classical buildings that they rarely if ever stop to admire them. The beautiful Sessions House, which opened in 1884, dominates the left of the view as we look towards Commutation Row, with the Walker Art Gallery, the Central Library and Liverpool Museum nearby. Sadly, the other buildings in this view have long since been demolished. Rushworth & Dreaper was a high-class music shop well known to all Liverpool's music lovers who might have bought a piano or a radiogram there, and almost certainly at some time a record. Rushworth & Dreaper's prominent advert for His Master's Voice records is one of the 20th Century's most well known trademarks. The small dog in HMV's well-known ad was Nipper, whose master, the English painter Francis Barraud borrowed a gramophone with a large horn so that he could paint his dog alongside it. The Gramophone Company ended up buying the picture and adopted it as their trademark. The company later became RCA Victor and continued to use Nipper, who has ended up as possibly the most famous dog in the world. Towards the right of the photograph - dated 1947 - lies the Steble Fountain and St George's Hall.

Above right: As we look along Lord Street towards Church Street we can see that the area still bore its wartime scars in 1949; the programme of rebuilding was already in force, but there was still a long way to go before new buildings would cover these tracts of open ground. The new bus station would eventually be built near Paradise Street, while in time the building which now takes up the foreground of this shot would house the Blood Donor centre, the offices of the Automobile Association, and an office equipment store. Spot the premises of Boodle and Dunthorne on the left of the photograph; if called upon to do so, readers might still be able to sing their jolly little advertising jingle (though they would probably prefer not to!). A jingle of quite a different kind is connected with Paradise Street, linked to the old sea shanty 'Blow the Man Down'. Paradise Street is today home to Radio Merseyside, and the prestigious Moat House Hotel, while off-picture to the right lies the Seamen's Mission.

There was little traffic around in Clayton Square when the photographer captured this pigeon's eye view some time in 1947. Vehicles were obviously allowed to travel in both directions at the time, though this section of roadway later became part of the one-way system. The square has long been a lively shopping centre with many small shops and department stores. Redevelopment during the 1960s changed the face of Clayton Square forever - readers will surely remember St John's Market with a twinge of nostalgia. The superb complex of shops and services that replaced the old buildings still bustles with shoppers. Though the assault on the city removed beautiful buildings which can never be replaced, the tastefully-built shopping precinct is nevertheless appreciated by many, particularly parents who have buggies to push and small children to keep an eye on. Shoppers can today browse in comfort and safety, and after a hard morning are able to rest their tired feet in the centre's cafe area. If they are lucky, perhaps they can even enjoy their coffee and cakes to the accompaniment of live piano music!

Above: A blast from the past for those who remember Lime Street and St George's Place before the planning department got busy with their red pens! The Royal Hotel on the far left helped to slake the thirst of Liverpudlians for many years - and you may remember calling in at the Savoy on the next corner for a pint or two in your younger days - both gone from the scene now along with the entire row of buildings. Gone too is the old St George's Hotel and the row of shops on the right, destined to be eventually replaced by a new hotel of the same name. The beginning of the 21st century saw the hotel closed as teams of workers moved in to carry out extensive renovations and improvements to the building. How many readers remember holding hands on the back row of the ABC Forum in the background of this nostalgic shot? Many happy evenings have been spent there over the years as we lost ourselves in the magic of the silver screen! Motor car buffs will enjoy this glance back at the cars we drove in 1960, from the old Standard Vanguard Mk II, distinguished by its squared-off boot (the Mk I had a sloping back) to the Vauxhall Wyvern facing it. Spot the relatively rare German Opel.

Below: This would appear to be a photograph of an accident about to happen, as a jay-walking pedestrian steps out boldly across Lord Street and risks being knocked down by an oncoming 6A tram. We can only hope that this gentleman lived to jay-walk another day and did not become part of the city's accident statistics!

The year was 1955, and within a couple of years the roar of the diesel bus was to take over from the tramway network. Ten years after the end of the second world war Liverpool was still replacing buildings which were destroyed in bombing raids, and we can see that reconstruction is underway on the left. The new buildings which emerged were all harsh angles and squares, sadly characterless in comparison with the elegant structures they replaced. The large advert on J & F Stone's electrical shop promoting Atlas lamps will be familiar to more mature readers - the same happy light bulb stared down at us from many a wall during the 1940s. By that time, of course, the majority of householders had installed electricity, though many homes were still lit by gas until well into the 1940s.

Both pictures: Lime Street did not have today's volume of traffic back in 1952, the date of this photograph, and the bus shelters which occupy the foreground, spoiling our view of the Plateau, demonstrates the principal method of travelling into the city and home again *(below)*. The statue of the Duke of Wellington, in the right background (and bombarded every day by pigeons), has long been a well-known landmark in the city. Wellington and Napoleon met in battle near Waterloo on 18th June 1815; the battle was by no means an easy one but

Wellington proved to be more than a match for Napoleon. The guns captured at Waterloo were melted down and provided the material for this impressive 132ft high statue, and the grand charge at Waterloo is celebrated in relief on the plinth.

St Georges Plateau has rightly been named one of the city's finest sights, a work of art in itself. Even Queen Victoria - reputedly not easily amused - pronounced this spot as being worthy of Athens. Her statue, depicting Victoria mounted on horseback,

was erected in St George's Plateau in 1870, and is balanced by a similar one of her consort Prince Albert. After the first world war the beautiful and intensely moving cenotaph was erected at the foot of St George's Hall steps; a memorial in bronze relief depicts the men who fought and fell, and the mourners who were left behind. The Plateau has been the scene of many ceremonies and events, so we cannot be sure what the occasion was which called for the procession holding up the Lime Street traffic in our second photograph *(bottom)*. There are no uniforms among the marchers, so this is not a military parade. Perhaps our readers can shed some light on the mystery?

From his vantage point 132 feet above St George's Plateau, the Duke of Wellington solemnly contemplates the scene below - perhaps, we might think, disapproving the cluttering up of the Plateau with motor cars. Lovers of trivia will enjoy hearing that in addition to bequeathing his name to the humble welly the great man was also an early patron of the umbrella, and his patronage did much to enhance its popularity. Umbrellas were not considered modish until around 1800, but thereafter they became fashion accessories for gentlemen. Indeed, so indispensable were they

that - so the story goes - British officers, while under fire at Bayonne, put their umbrellas up to keep their uniforms dry. But a message came from the Duke of Wellington to say that he did 'not approve of the use of umbrellas during the enemy's firing and will not allow gentlemen's sons to make themselves ridiculous in the eyes of the army.'

Set into the flight of steps that leads up to the pillared loggia of St George's Hall, the Earl of Beaconsfield looks towards the rather beautiful, if incongruously coffin-like, cenotaph, which was erected in 1930 to remember those who lost their lives in the Great War.

This page: Day gives way to night in these contrasting shots of St George's Crescent back in 1957. How different things look at dusk, when the illuminated clock on the Imperial Hotel and the neon advertising all around bring sparkle and life to the very ordinary scene, turning the area into a fairyland of light and colour! There was a good selection of entertainment along this stretch of roadway, from watching a marionette show or a game of snooker to an evening spent ballroom dancing. The brilliant signs show us that each hotel plugs its favoured drink; The Washington pushes Martel Brandy, St George's advises VP wine, while the Imperial goes all the way, reminding passers by that Guinness was good for them every time they glanced up to check their watches against the clock which gave them 'Guinness time'. The British have believed that Guinness was good for them since the drink was first advertised in 1929. When they decided to advertise, Arthur Guinness & Son called in some consumer research experts to help them with the ads. The experts found that many of the punters believed it did them good - and the first Guinness slogan, 'Guinness is so Strengthening' was born. Many clever slogans have been produced over the years: 'Tall, Dark and Have Some', 'Seven Million Every Day and Still Going Down' and notably 'I've Never Tried it Because I Don't Like it'. And remember 'Guinness is Good for you - Just think what Toucan do'?

Below: It was the genius of the youthful architect Harvey Lonsdale Elmes which gave the city St George's Hall, the undoubted jewel in Liverpool's crown and famous even further afield, being described as the finest neo-classical building in Europe. The 23-year-old Elmes's design was chosen by competition. The young man, however, was suffering from 'consumption', the scourge of the 19th century. He spent some time abroad, but even the pleasant climate of the West Indies failed to cure his tuberculosis, and he died before he could see his masterpiece completed in 1854.

Facing St George's Hall across Lime Street stands the 330 room, turreted North Western Hotel - an elegant building built in 1871. Originally well-used by travellers arriving at the adjoining Lime Street Station, the building is today used as student accommodation for John Moore's University. The Empire Theatre in the left foreground, still the largest two-tier theatre in Britain,

opened under the rather grand name of the Royal Alexandra Theatre and Opera House in July 1867. Since then, the feet of many of the famous have trodden its boards, including such old-time legends as Sarah Bernhardt and Vesta Tilley. After extensive renovation the theatre re-opened as the Empire on 19th December 1896 - just in time for the children of Liverpool to enjoy the pantomime 'Cinderella'.

Bottom: This is one photograph where we might wish for colour film to have been used; the tubs of flowers in the foreground would have made a beautiful display. The photograph, dated 1960, was taken from Manchester Street. There has been a 'Mitre' public house on this spot in Dale Street for many years, and the pub still survives. Today officially named The Ship and Mitre, its old name is good enough for its regular patrons! The local brewery Bents - well known for

supplying the cheapest beer in the city - was founded in Scotland Road in 1810 by Richard Bent, later operating from various other sites. The brewery, by that time in Johnson Street, was taken over by Bass Charrington in 1967. It was during the 1960s that DIY began to take a firm foothold with young couples who wanted to create their 'dream home', and Robinson & Neal Ltd, to the right of the photograph, would perhaps have been the young enthusiast's first port of call. The late 18th century building - one of the city's finest - here displays the prominent adverts for Ripolin paints and the well-known Crown products. These merchant's houses came through the war and still survive today.

This page: Exactly ten years after the end of the second world war South Castle Street and Lord Street had still some way to go to full recovery after the hammering they took during the Blitz *(right)*. Gangs of construction workers had moved in and over the following few years Derby Square, Lord Street and South Castle Street were transformed as new buildings rose, floor by floor, from their foundations. The contrasting shot, *(bottom)* taken in 1963, shows us the progress which had already been made. A rather long zebra crossing spans the square; readers may remember that crossings were only given their zebra stripes in 1951, though pedestrian crossings, marked out by studs and yellow beacons, were introduced back in 1934. The very first beacons were made of glass - irresistible to small boys with a destructive streak, so the glass beacons were replaced by painted aluminium. In 1952 the globes became plastic and began to wink.

The Victoria Monument in Derby Square, and its shallow steps, just creep into the lower right of both photographs. The monument itself, erected in

1906, escaped the worst of the bombing which flattened the surrounding buildings and turned the area into a wasteland. This particular site has seen more momentous changes than most places over the years. Back in the days of King John a castle, complete with moat, stood here. It was demolished in 1721 and St George's church built in its place. The church in turn was pulled down just before the turn of the 20th century.

Above: Doesn't it seem a long time since motorists were able to enjoy driving along a clear and uncongested road? The rather nice building on the right is the Botanical Gardens' Lodge, and further away, the gardens themselves. Around the bend in Edge Lane, readers can perhaps pick out the huge Littlewoods Pools building, whose size reflects the popularity of 'doing the pools'. Founded by Sir John Moores, a former chairman of Everton FC, Littlewoods achieved fame and made a number of fortunes over the years. On the day this view was recorded in 1957, Edge lane (pockmarked as a result of road works of one kind and another) was all but deserted. But things were about to change in a big way. By the late 1950s post war prosperity was creating a new consumer market, and for the first time the ordinary person in the street had the money to spend on luxury goods such as washing machines, fridges - and motor cars, which would soon rule supreme on the city's roads. Later that same year, the humble tram, still running along Edge Lane at the time, would itself reach the end of the line.

Top: The supplanter and the supplanted in one shot! Buses were destined to replace Liverpool's electric railway system in the not too distant future, though back in 1948 the driver of this Number 79 bus would have had no idea that the overhead railway, so much a part of Liverpool life, would one day be replaced by buses. If he had, he would no doubt have been astounded, as a bus journey of an hour and a quarter was necessary to cover the distance from Seaforth Sands to Dingle - a trip the train could make in less than 25 minutes! Diesel buses were brought in to replace the overhead railway in December 1956 - a few weeks after the Suez crisis began and Liverpool became dependent on fuel from the Middle East. What planner of old do we have to thank for this example of clarity of thought? It was not only the dockers who would miss the good old 'Dockers' Umbrella' as they took advantage of its shelter from the elements on their daily walk to work. A trip on the overhead railway was a real experience for young and old alike, who were treated to those marvellous views of the huge ocean liners, the dash and drive of the docks - and a panorama that spanned the Mersey to the seaside resort of New Brighton. Note the number of buildings surrounded by scaffolding in this shot, as post-war rebuilding gathered momentum.

Bottom: Tram lines in the foreground of this 1956 shot of London Road and Pembroke Place indicate the meeting and parting of the ways. A few short months on, it would be the parting of the ways for Liverpool and the last of its tram routes, and those magnificent old Green Goddesses and Baby Grands would be sent on to that great tram shed in the sky. As we look towards the statue of the inappropriately toga-clad King George III in Monument Place (designed by Robert Westmacott), T J Hughes department store lies off to the left. The statue's plinth bears the legend 'Erected by Public Subscription'; is there any truth, we wonder, in the rumour that the monies received were not sufficient to dress His Majesty in the robes which would perhaps have been more appropriate to his kingship? We draw a veil over such speculation, though George III, whose illness made him rather eccentric from time to time, was not everyone's favourite monarch....

Right: Think of Scotland Road at one time, and the very name would conjure up images of towering, overcrowded tenements, narrow streets, dismal back alleys, poor housing, and grinding poverty. Often overlooked is the other aspect of Scotland Road; the community spirit, the friendliness of neighbours who were always ready to step in with the loan of a cup of sugar in an emergency or a little sympathetic help and advice in a family crisis. This was all destined to change as clearance schemes wiped out whole communities during the 1950s and 60s. At the time, women must have longed with all their souls for somewhere better to bring up their young families.

The new housing provided modern facilities for many people who had to wash in the scullery and share an outside lavatory with a couple of other families. For the first time they had modern bathrooms with a wash basin and an indoor loo, central heating, electric cookers and endless hot water. The facilities were great - but the community spirit they had enjoyed in the old Scotland Road had gone.

Younger readers will enjoy the unfamiliar sight of buses, cars, lorries and jay walkers in Church Street in those long ago days before pedestrianisation transformed the bustling shopping area into a haven, if not of peace then at least of comparative safety. Changes were afoot, however, long before the date of this photograph - St Peter's church, remembered only by a plaque set into the pavement, once formed part of this view; the white building in the right background replaced it. As long as Liverpudlians can remember (and further back still), Church Street has been one of the city's main shopping streets. Church

Street's claim to fame is as the location of the very first Woolworth's store in Britain. It was here that Frank Winfield Woolworth's 'Nothing over 6d' policy set his feet firmly on the road to country-wide fame and fortune. The Woolworths '3d and 6d Stores' were a direct echo of the original '5 and 10 cent Stores' that spread in a chain across America at the end of the 19th Century. F W Woolworth, who in 1879 opened his first stores selling a wide range of goods at fixed low prices, had a chain of over 1,000 shops in the USA by 1911. With his brother C S Woolworth he later expanded into the UK, Canada and Europe.

By the Mersey

The sight of a brand new ocean-going liner alongside the landing stage has always presented an awesome sight, and a crowd has gathered to watch as the dazzling white Reina del Mar, dwarfing its little tugs, docks in Liverpool on 9th April 1956. Among them is a photographer who has set up his camera and tripod to record the event. Where are his photographs now, we wonder? Captain Rice and his chief engineer Mr Currie together made a team as good as any Tikka Masala as the sleek and elegant £5m vessel arrived in the Mersey straight from the yards of Harland and Wolff in Belfast. The 600ft long Reina del Mar could offer three classes of accommodation, with 207 first class, 216 cabin class and 343 tourist class cabins. In addition eight de-luxe twin-bed cabins were on offer, each with individual decor. First class passengers could enjoy a screened-off, 24ft open air swimming pool, a sports deck and special facilities for children, including a play room and paddling pool. The ship's cinema was even equipped to show the Cinemascope films which enjoyed huge popularity during the 1950s, and when necessary it doubled as a dance hall. An evocative glance back through the years!

liner holidaymakers could enjoy the cruise of a lifetime, whether they were looking for peace and quiet, good food and pleasant company, or plenty of dancing, fun and gaiety. The days when we could enjoy the sight of several big liners in the Mersey at one time are sadly long gone - though well remembered.

Top: The overhead railway bisects this 1936 view from left to right; riding on the 'overhead' was quite an experience - readers will remember the marvellous rooftop level views of Liverpool's busy dockland. The first stretch of the Liverpool Overhead Railway, between Herculaneum Dock in the south to Alexandra Dock in the north, opened in 1893. It proved popular not only with seamen and dockers but also with visitors, and the following year it was extended northwards to the residential areas of Seaforth and Waterloo, and southwards to Dingle. The docks, of course, were a prime target of Nazi bombing raids and Liverpool suffered badly during the second world war. Liverpudlians will recognise Canning Dock on the left and Salthouse on the right, and the long lines of dock sheds along the waterfront. Behind them stands the imposing Customs House. Time and redevelopment was to bring enormous changes to the area, though the dock sheds which lie off the photograph to the right were preserved for posterity. Albert Dock, in the right foreground, has become a major tourist attraction. Readers will pick out the Maritime Museum and the Granada Television studios.

Above: A sight to stir the blood as well as the many memories of the hundreds of huge passenger liners which once used to come into Liverpool. Among them, over the years, have been many famous names: MV Britannic, the Aquitania, RMS Mauretania, the Empress of Canada. Tragedy was connected with some, such as RMS Lusitania, which was torpedoed by a German submarine during the first world war off southern Ireland. More than 1,000 people lost their lives. But another war had been fought and won when a photographer recorded this marvellous shot of the Franconia in 1948. Along with the Ascania, she offered a regular cross-Atlantic service to Canada. Aboard the elegant

Above: This marvellous gull's eye view of Gladstone Dock was shot in 1952, capturing for posterity the hustle and bustle of the city's dock life. When permission was granted for the dock system to be extended to the north of the Liverpool Dock Estate, the first phase in the construction of Gladstone Dock began. A graving dock - a dry dock where ships could be repaired - was developed ahead of the main scheme, and was opened by King George V on 11th July 1913. Gladstone Dock was the largest graving dock in Europe. A year later, however, the Great War broke out, interrupting the new development. Construction eventually went ahead and nine years after in July 1927 the King, accompanied by Queen Mary, returned to Liverpool to declare the entire Gladstone Dock officially open. The royal couple were entertained to lunch at the Town Hall before boarding the Harbour Board vessel Galatea at the Princes Landing Stage. They sailed down the river and into the Gladstone Lock, where they ceremonially cut the ribbon across the entrance.

Below: A consignment of American cars are being unloaded at Liverpool Pierhead in this splendid photograph - which nevertheless is a rather ironic sight. The scene was snapped back in 1951, when British industry was exporting as much as it could, and our own motor industry was enjoying particular success in marketing its cars abroad. In the aftermath of the second world war, Britain's priority was to rebuild its economy, which meant that all sectors of British industry had to concentrate heavily on the export market. At the same time, the Buy British campaign was in full swing to encourage us all to buy goods made by British manufacturers in preference to those of foreign competitors wherever possible. The Festival of Britain took place in the same year as our picture, and, with its many high-profile trade exhibitions and events held all over the country providing a platform for British manufacturers, was designed to restore confidence in British industry.

Asolitary man slowly makes his way up the Floating Road in a photograph which contrasts strongly with many old pictures which show scenes of congested traffic queuing to load and unload from the luggage boats. The road, a superb example of engineering, was designed to cope with traffic at any time, and rose and fell with the tide. Readers may remember the steep incline when the tide was out. The photographer captured a particularly quiet time; we can see that a good number of buses are standing in the terminal, though there are few passengers waiting to board them.

Dominating the scene, of course, is the Royal Liver Building, whose impressive clock, set 220ft above ground level, informs us that it is 3.45pm. The average passer-by is unlikely to think of the size of the four clockfaces, but with a diameter of 25ft it is considerably larger than that of Big Ben. Each of the minute hands is an incredible 14ft in length! The clock - at the time, the largest electrically operated clock in Britain, was started up on 22nd June 1911. The building's mythical Liver Birds, instantly recognisable even to visitors to Liverpool, are manufactured from copper and stand 18ft high.

Out & about

Below: *Are these two young ladies fortunate enough to be visiting the Atlantic Club - or are they merely passing by? The Atlantic Club in Hardman Street will be remembered by many Liverpudlians who enjoyed dancing there in days long ago. The Atlantic was much more than your average 'drop in' facility; visits to this naval club were by invitation only and it was recognised as attracting a respectable class of people. This was a favourite venue with nurses from the Royal Children's Hospital, the*

Liverpool Radium Institute and the Ear, Nose and Throat Hospital, and their fathers could perhaps relax a little when they knew that their daughters were associating with a 'nice' set of friends. Not too far away - and still open today - is the Philharmonic pub, noted for its luxurious Victorian grandeur. Not too many pubs are famous for their toilet facilities (at least, not in a positive sense!), but the Philharmonic's very grand loos are known across the city for their rich splendour - especially the Gents!

With a little imagination you could fancy that at any minute you might be showered with arrows from the narrow loopholes of these twin turrets, or worse still with a couple of buckets of boiling oil from one of the windows. But after all, this 'medieval castle' with its archway and ornate fenestration is only the entrance to the Methodist Central Hall, whose walls have echoed to many years of sermons and lectures, hymns and Christmas carols. Closer inspection reveals the posters advertising forthcoming events which have been posted outside the doorway. It would be interesting to be able to read them and find out exactly what concerts and meetings were on the programme for that particular week back in 1963! Renovations to the building were to follow, but the Central Hall was built to last, and last it has - it is as much used today as ever. Perhaps an even greater range of functions is held within its walls today, and the craft fair - badge of the late 20th and early 21st century - is alive and well in the Central Hall and includes stamps, antiques, books and hand-made crafts.

Left: There were as many men as women in the queue outside St George's Hall when the Ideal Home Exhibition came to town. We have no date for this memorable picture, though the rising hemlines and swing-back coats point to the late 1950s. Hats, as we can see, were still in vogue at the time for men as well as women. The good old trilby was to virtually vanish not too far ahead. The fascinating notice board promises a great day out, with cooking demonstrations, a photographic quiz with a £20 prize (a sum really worth winning back then!), a cafe and a licensed bar. And who were the amazing Arvins? Do any of our readers remember seeing these 'mentalists with a difference'? Whatever the act was, the Arvins certainly earned their money as they offered 'continuous performances daily'! Some of the ladies in the queue had prudently brought along their shopping bags, as all the gadgets on display could be purchased from the exhibition. We can scarcely believe that all this was on offer for the price of a shilling (5p)! Those were the days!

Above: Were you among this crowd of people expectantly lining the pavements in Church Street back in 1939? If so, you will no doubt recall the occasion. Our only information about this shot is that a royal visit was expected, and a little detective work reveals that the Duke and Duchess of Kent visited Liverpool that year to unveil statues of King George V and Queen Mary. The King and Queen had visited Liverpool on a number of occasions, but the most important visit of all had been that made in 1934, when they officially declared open the Mersey Tunnel, described by many as the eighth wonder of the world. Thousands of proud Liverpudlians descended on the city centre, all eager to catch a glimpse of the royal couple. Among them, of course, were Liverpool's school children, who were all given a medal to mark the occasion. How many of them survive, we wonder, tucked away in boxes around the city? After the ceremony, the King was given a model of the tunnel entrance. King George V died in 1936, though his widow, Queen Mary, lived on until 1953.

Above: Entertaining Liverpudlians for decades, the extravagantly named Palais de Luxe was once one of our favourite cinemas. When it opened back in 1908 it was the Grand Tivoli theatre, though just three years on it was to change its name and convert to a cinema. Live music accompanied the silent films of the day, closely following the on-screen pathos or the fast moving action. But the Palais de Luxe saw in the advent of the 'talkies' in 1929 - the wonder technology of the day. In many places, special trains were laid on to take cinemagoers to shed romantic tears over Jolson's rendering of 'Danny Boy' in 'The Singing Fool'. 'Danny Boy' was of course destined to become everyone's favourite song. A disastrous fire in 1951 called for extensive rebuilding. But the 1950s saw declining audiences in all our cinemas as the small screen in the corner of everyone's living room gradually took hold, and at the time of our photograph the Palais de Luxe had already shown its last film. It closed in 1959 and was replaced by the shops we know today. The Forum, to the right of the shot, opened in 1931 and lived through many changes of name. By the end of the century it was to lie empty and unused.

Above right: It needs no Sherlock Holmes to deduce that as this view of Goodison Park is dated 1957 - the year the pitch's floodlighting system was set up - it would have been a commemorative photograph. The powerful floodlights were installed to mark the anniversary of the Liverpool County FA on 9th October 1957; were any of our readers in the crowd when they were switched on for the

game played against Liverpool? Goodison Park has been home to Everton FC since the club bought an overgrown field near Goodison Road back in 1892, with the aid of an interest-free loan from a member. No time was lost in transforming the wilderness into a satisfactory football ground with a covered stand, two uncovered stands, gates, sheds and turnstiles, and FA officials Lord Kinnaird and Frederick Wall declared the ground officially open on 24th August that same year. Many star players have emerged from Everton FC since that day: centre forwards Alex Young and Joe Royle - and the amazing William Ralph 'Dixie' Dean, who in 29 League games scored an incredible 60 League goals (a record which, at the time of writing, has not been broken); 31 in 15 away games, and 29 in 14 home matches.

Below centre: The dull, damp weather underlines the unlovely surroundings and bleak aspect which characterised Shaw Street back in 1952, where smart houses and the not so smart rubbed shoulders with each other, and the odd broken window went unnoticed. To many Liverpudlians, this long row of grim housing was home. There were once hundreds of other such streets around the city, and many of them have gone forever. Former residents, however, speak more of the amazing sense of community and friendship than of their dreary surroundings. What were these two little girls waiting for when a passing photographer saw the potential beauty of the image he caught on film, we wonder? And what memories of their home would they share with us today? The children's dress is typical of the early 1950s; countless readers will remember the ankle socks which a decade further on would be replaced by white knee socks. The smaller of the two girls - sisters, maybe? - has her little handbag with her - her first concession to growing up! It is interesting to note the lack of television aerials on the chimneys; TV was popularised by the Queen's coronation in 1953.

Bottom: A long-established tradition all across Britain was at one time that of the weekly wash, and Monday mornings started early for the housewife, whose task it was to keep her family clean and decent. There were beds to be stripped, the copper to be lit and the tub to be filled before the gruelling job could be started. The end of the day saw exhausted women, their hands reddened by the hot water, the rubbing board and the mangle, who still had to prepare a meal for their menfolk to come home to. For the benefit of younger readers who have grown up with automatic washing machines and tumble dryers, a mangle was to their grandmothers an indispensable part of washday equipment. The housewife (yes, never the men!) would squeeze the water out of wet washing between the mangle's heavy wooden rollers - and winding the handle that turned the rollers was hard work.

A neatly wrapped package of success

The Liverpool company, Smith and Bateson Limited is one of the UK's largest paper and polythene distributors with an interesting history that dates back over two centuries, to the year, 1801.

The history of paper making itself, in this country, dates back over 500 years. However, it was not until the 18th Century that there were any great number of mills. It was towards the end of the 1700s that the demand for paper began to exceed the supply and as a result, many enterprising people of vision became interested and involved in the paper trade.

One of these aforementioned enterprising people of vision was William Bateson, a builder by trade. However, his interest and involvement in the paper trade extended to actually building a paper mill. This

mill was located in Matshead near Preston in Lancashire, and was completed in 1801. Its completion marked the foundation of the company that was later to be known as Smith and Bateson Limited. The initial function of the new business was that of making wrapping paper.

Above left: Mr William Smith, who joined Roger Bateson as partner in 1855.
Below: Pitt Street in 1934. *Above:* From top left, clockwise: Robert Smith, R.P. Smith, J.D. Smith.

At the time, this process was a long and arduous one. Indeed, it almost seems unimaginable when compared to today's standards, that it used to take William Bateson two days to bring a ton of paper from the mill to Liverpool. He travelled in a stiff cart without springs and used to have to stop off for the night at a public house in Burscough beyond Ormskirk called the Bull and Dog. On delivering the paper he exchanged it for a ton of rags which he would then take back to the mill via the same route to make some more paper.

William's fledgling business proved to be a success and it was not long before it became a family run firm. William had seven children, four boys and three girls. Two of his sons went into the church and one died at a young age. It was therefore left to his son Roger to join the family business, and this he did, in 1832, working at the Matshead mill. Meanwhile, one of William's daughters, Mary, married Thomas Whitby, a Spice Merchant from Liverpool with a mill situated in Seel Street. Sadly, Thomas' business failed and soon after, he died. Mary and her children were left on their own and so returned to Matshead. Thanks to her father's generosity it was not long before Mary was able to go back to Liverpool. William bought a shop at 41 Pitt Street and stocked it with all sorts of paper products for Mary, who returned to Liverpool to run it. The opening of the shop marked the beginning of the merchanting side of what was soon to become the Smith and Bateson concern.

Above: The Pitt Street premises' entrance in 1943. From left to right: Joe Mather, Arthur Rushton, David Welch.

The Pitt Street shop soon began to flourish and when Mary eventually retired, her eldest son, William Bateson Whitby took over the running of the business. Sadly, in 1859, following an accident, William Bateson Whitby died. His younger brother Thomas was expected to carry on the concern but he decided instead, to go into the church. The merchanting side of the business was a successful one and there was no question of abandoning it, a new successor needed to be found.

It was eventually decided that the founders' son, Roger Bateson should move from the Matshead mill to Liverpool and run the merchanting business. Mary's sister Alice had married Thomas Smith of Goosenargh, also a builder and it was decided that their eldest son, William Smith should join his Uncle Roger in running the shop. Subsequently, Roger and William became partners in the merchanting business. When they took over the running of the shop, the business became known as Whitby, Bateson & Smith and was valued at £3700. This money had been lent by the Whitby family at 5 per cent and, in fact, it took until 1865 to pay the family back upon which time, the business was renamed Smith & Bateson.

William Smith decided that he would undertake travelling. Once again someone else was needed to take charge of the shop. This time, John Bateson, Roger Bateson's son, was appointed this task. By then, the business, still small, operated chiefly as a retail counter trade selling such things as, writing paper, envelopes and coloured tissue paper bought by a lot of women who made a living by making fire-grate papers.

The orders were all sent out by hand-cart to shops in town and, to keep down expenses, no horses were used, instead orders for the country were taken to the station by two porters, James and Jennings.

Trade picked up again and consequently, more help was needed. Robert Smith, William's brother, was invited to leave Goosenargh and come to Liverpool. This he did and in his own words said that at first, "A hard life it was. The three of us lived with an old person at 2 Ivy Street, had a back parlour and one bedroom. She kept a pig in the yard, so you see we did not start life in style". Time went on and the old lady died, so the men moved to 104 Canning Street where they stayed until William married Ellen Crankshaw and bought 127 Canning Street. William and Ellen had four children, Thomas Bateson Smith, William Ernest Smith,

In the early 1900s the paper mill at Matshead was closed and the firm began to concentrate on the Liverpool business

Richard Percy Smith and Hilda Smith. Sadly, William died in 1883 when his children were still infants and 'Uncle Robert Smith' became the beloved father figure of his three young nephews as well as taking charge of Smith & Bateson.

Under Robert Smith's guidance, Smith & Bateson continued successfully, for years of steady growth and development. In 1890, his nephew, Thomas Bateson Smith joined the business followed by William Ernest Smith in 1892 and Richard Percy Smith in 1894. Mr R.P. (as he was known) was a committed Everton fan and even though he worked at Smith & Bateson until half past two on Saturday

Top: *A horse owned by the company in the 1920s that won the Challenge Cup in the Liverpool Parade of Horses. With the horse is Jock Barrett, the senior carter.*

afternoons he never missed a home match. When they were playing at home he used to run from Pitt Street to catch a tram and managed to get to Everton in time for the kick off. John Bateson, known as Johnny, had become a partner at around the time Mr R.P. joined the firm and he remembered him as a bachelor, very good with horses, both riding and driving a carriage, but very mean about money. He used to send Mr R.P. to buy matches from a shop half a mile away because there, they sold 13 boxes of matches for one penny rather than the usual 12 boxes! John never used to take any holidays and Mr R.P. used to say that this was because he was afraid he would not be missed. Another story told about him was that when the clerks complained that it was cold in the office he used to reply, "Write faster and keep yourself warm"!

In contrast, Mr R.P. had fond memories of Robert Smith. He was a talented amateur pianist and organist and was well known in Liverpool musical circles. His Uncle Robert even asked him if he wanted to leave Smith & Bateson's to become a professional musician. However, Mr R.P. decided that he wanted to stay, a decision he never regretted, especially as his eyesight started to deteriorate when he reached his 30s. Because of his deteriorating eyesight Mr R.P. had to start walking with a stick and this fact ensured that he became a well known figure in Pitt Street and the adjacent area where the children would call out cheerily, "Hello Mr Smitty-Bate"! Another fond memory of Uncle Robert was from the dance he gave for his daughter's birthday at the Adelphi Hotel in Liverpool around 1910. When the band started to play he called the head waiter over and said they were not playing with much sparkle and would he give them a glass of champagne. The head waiter is reputed to have said, "That's not usual Sir" and Uncle Robert replied, "We Smiths are not usual people"! Anyway, they were given a glass of champagne each and apparently played much better!

Above left: *An early ½ lb sugar bag, the smallest size produced by the company.*
Below: *The first van owned by the company after the war, with driver, Joe Mather. The picture dates from the late 1940s.*

In the early 1900s the paper mill at Matshead closed down and the firm's concentration turned solely to the thriving merchanting business in Liverpool. By this time the business had grown to such an extent that the storage offered by the shop was no longer adequate. Consequently, Smith & Bateson built a new four storey warehouse in Pitt Street at a cost of £2,348. In 1912, a week before his 14th birthday, Tom Parrott joined the firm and later, his wife and two sisters were among the 40 'girls' employed in the bag room making hand made bags. The hours were 8 am to 6 pm at a wage of 2/6d and any who were late were fined a quarter of the days wages. At that time there were eight men in the warehouse and their foreman, Mr Taylor, was known as 'Major'! Jack Barrett was the firm's senior carter and like the rest of his drivers wore white canvas aprons and riding breeches. In fact, the carters won the Liverpool Tradesmen's Turnout for a total of six years! They started work at seven am and there was no overtime even though they fed and looked after the horses at weekends and Bank Holidays. There were two wagons and three horses. The horses too, worked hard. They crossed the Mersey on the ferry to deliver in Birkenhead and Wallasey and had to lie down on the deck in a storm. One horse, Jerry, was once hit on the nose by a tram car in Longmoor Lane. In bad weather sacking was wrapped over the horses hooves prompting questions such as, "Is that to keep their feet warm?"!

It was also at around this time that the firm's association with the Cathrell family first began. The first member of the Cathrell family joined the firm as a coachman driving a brougham as well as being in charge of buying the horses from a farm near Preston. He always walked the horses back to Liverpool from the farm near Preston as he would not let them endure the stress of a train ride. His son Tom joined the firm as a traveller before the second

Above: The company celebrated 150 years in business in 1951. This brochure dates from that time.
Below: One of the company's 1960s fleet.

world war and, in turn, his son, Raymond also joined the company and worked as sales manager before retiring in 1987.

It was not until after the first world war that the firm was able to purchase its first car, a Meteorite with brass fittings. This was followed a year later with the purchase of a Thorneycroft. It was also at about this time that Smith & Bateson won an important contract with Tate & Lyle. The firm was contracted to make strong dark blue bags for the company's sugar. However after many years, without any warning, Tate and Lyle cancelled the order as they decided to use cardboard cartons instead. Despite this, Smith & Bateson won other contracts and continued to flourish.

The 1930s proved to be an eventful decade for Pitt Street itself. For years goods were passed through the windows at the four storey warehouse and manhandled up a wooden staircase. Eventually, however a manually operated outside lift was installed. The warehouse was also occupied by the police during the early 1930s when they asked if two detectives could hide there to keep watch on a suspected opium den nearby. This watch lasted for over a week before the police were able to make any arrests! Also, on a lighter note, on the occasion of King George V's Silver Jubilee, the residents of the Pitt Street tenements won an award for their street decorations.

Sadly, in 1931, Robert Smith died. However, this meant that he was saved the distress of having to reduce the wages of his workforce during the depression of the 1930s. This job was left to Richard Percy Smith. The value of paper had fallen to pre-war levels whilst expenses and wages were more than twice as much as at pre-war levels. Richard did not want to loose any of his staff so sent out a letter asking them if they would manage with lower wages so that the business could continue. Fortunately, this was agreed to and Smith & Bateson managed to stay in business. In 1934, Richard Percy's son, John Denis Smith joined the firm after leaving school. Four years later, in 1938, the senior carter, Jack Barrett had an accident and was not able to work. Consequently, the horses were discontinued and to compensate, Tom Parrot learned how to drive and the firm bought another motor van.

The advent of the second world war prolonged the difficulties at Smith & Bateson, but despite his ill health, Mr R.P. managed to keep the firm going throughout the hostilities. Before war was declared, the Liverpool Council decided to redevelop the Pitt Street area. This meant knocking down the firm's warehouse and office. Mr R.P. did not want to move

Above: *Retired staff at the 'moving party' in July 1970. From left to right: Ada Mercer, Florie Lumberg, JD Smith, Gladys Littlewood, Arthur Rushton, Mr & Mrs Tom Parrot.*

and the Town Clerk suggested that the compensation money would persuade him as he was only in business for the money. RP was devoted to his staff and their families and was insulted by this comment. Fortunately however, the scheme was shelved when war was declared.

At the declaration of war, the paper trade was immediately governed by the Paper Control. As a paper merchant, the firm had to make a return of the amount of paper it had purchased in the previous year and on that basis was allocated a tonnage to purchase from British mills. The importation of paper was no longer allowed. Consequently, there was a shortage of paper, mainly, greaseproof paper. Most mills started using recycled paper but by the end of the war the quality was very poor.

During the Liverpool Blitz most of the buildings in Pitt Street were destroyed and every window in the warehouse was blown out. One of the firm's vans had been commandeered three days after the declaration of war to serve as an ambulance in Guilford. However, the firm's other vans were damaged by an incendiary bomb but fortunately, the warehouse and

The nature of the industry changed in the 1950s due to the advent of polythene

its workers survived. (Indeed, this solitary building became known as Stronghold House!) The decision was made to evacuate the office and all papers and documents to West Kirby where the business was run from Mr RP's dining room! His son Denis had joined the navy in the spring of 1940 but because Mr RP's health started to deteriorate, he was granted compassionate leave from the navy in 1945 in order to help run the business.

After the war, although the business was in a bad way, it had managed to survive intact and maintain trading. The Paper Control still remained in charge of almost all trade and in fact, it was not until 1952 that it finally ceased to function. The nature of the industry itself had also changed dramatically, especially due to the advent of polythene. However, Smith & Bateson summoned up its long history of experience and steady success and with it, gradually began to overcome the problems created by the depression and the war. The firm was quick to adapt to the changing nature of the industry and in the 1960s Smith & Bateson became one of the first firms to sell

Below: *Moving into the new factory in July 1970. From left to right: Billy Matthews, Steve O'Donnell, Joe Mather, Fred Scott, Charlie Edwards.*

the new material, HDPE to the butchery trade. It was also during this period, in 1964, that Mr. J.D. was appointed the Chairman of the National Association of Paper Merchants.

By 1970 the firm's turnover was growing rapidly and the business was thriving once again. This increased success meant that the Pitt Street warehouse had become too small to meet the needs of the expanding business. So, as a result, in 1970, the firm moved to a new 60000 square foot warehouse situated in Forth Street. To celebrate this move the firm held a party which was also attended by its retired staff.

Today, Smith & Bateson has become one of the UK's largest paper and polythene distributors. The company specialises in plain and printed, point of sale packaging for the retailer in a variety of materials including paper, high and low density polythene and nylon. The company now has an impressive portfolio including Supermarkets, Department Stores, Fashion Houses and Specialist Retailers as well as Packaging Merchants and Catering Organisations. The company stocks over 2000 competitively priced, high quality product lines and offers a nation-wide delivery service from its own fleet of vehicles. The ever expanding business has outgrown its premises in Forth Street and consequently, is planning to move to new and larger premises on a five and a half acre site situated in Knowsley. This move will, no doubt, develop the business even further and make it even more accessible to the whole of the United Kingdom.

Although the company's founding fathers would probably not recognise the new technology and even some of the new materials used in the business today, they would nevertheless find no change in the company's basic principles including innovation, flexibility and expertise. With yet another generation of Smiths - J.D.'s son, John Christopher Bateson Smith (current Chairman) and his son, Peter Smith - playing a part in the management team, the company's family tradition and wealth of experience and expertise persists. Indeed, the people at Smith & Bateson take pride in the fact that they have remained stable and carried steadily on for almost 200 years through booms and slumps and peace and war in order to continue to maintain a neatly wrapped package of success with an impressive longevity set to continue for many more years to come.

Above left: *One of the modern day fleet.*
Top: *The staff inside the new warehouse.*

Bird's eye view

The Cotton Exchange (centre of the photograph) was opened by the Prince of Wales (who four years later was to become King George V); with him was his wife, Princess Mary. Built at the height of Liverpool's booming trade in cotton, the Exchange was a magnificent building. Supporting the structure were 74 spectacular columns of royal pearl granite, quarried in Norway. The Exchange was a marvel of modern technology, and nothing that would facilitate the transaction of business was overlooked. Businessmen were provided with every facility they could possibly need; around the hall were side wings, with telephone boxes, postal and telegraph facilities and cable offices; even the flooring for the enormous hall was of noiseless rubber. Within the building were banking facilities, a clearing house, arbitration and appeal rooms and suites of cotton offices. The design for the Cotton Exchange was selected by competition; it is as well that the designer did not live to see the characterless facade which would one day replace his elegant frontage. The long rooftops of the well-remembered Exchange Station, built in 1850 for the Lancashire and Yorkshire Railway Company, lie to the left. The station closed in April 1977.

Rows of white sun blinds above the windows of the shops along London Road proclaim the fact that this bird's eye view was recorded on a warm, sunny day. A tram passes the fine Owen Owen department store; today the premises of T J Hughes, where you can buy anything from a dinner service to a pair of shoes. The store is still a firm favourite among Liverpool shoppers. Lovers of trivia will either remember or enjoy reading that just off to the right of the photograph lay Guyler's tailor's shop, a local business which had a family

connection with the famous personality Derek Guyler. Near Owen Owen stands the statue of George III, incongruously dressed in a toga and sandals; many changes have been made in London Road, but the statue remains.
A photograph taken from the same angle today would reveal a vastly changed scene. The red pen of the planners removed vast areas of residential housing, though one of the rows of buildings in the foreground has been preserved for posterity more or less in its original state - today used as office accommodation rather than as homes.

No book on nostalgic Liverpool would be complete without a photograph which included the impressive Anglican Cathedral, which has been very much a part of the life of the city since King Edward VII laid the foundation stone on 19th July 1904. The talented architect Sir Giles Gilbert Scott - who was himself a Roman Catholic - designed the cathedral at the amazing age of 21. The magnificent Lady Chapel was completed by 1910 and was used for worship until 1924. The building of the Cathedral turned out to be an ongoing project, however, and 74 years would go by before it was completed in October 1978. The Liverpool artist Edward Carter Preston executed most of the sculpture. The Cathedral is probably the most fitting place to remember those football fans who tragically lost their lives at Hillsbrough during the FA Cup Final in 1989, and a memorial plaque has been set into the floor on the steps of the Rankin Porch.

hat a wealth of city landmarks is contained in this one view! From this height we can fully appreciate St John's Garden, laid out to the rear of St George's Hall. The garden is named for the church which once stood on the spot; around 27,000 bodies were interred in St John's churchyard, and it's rather strange to think, as you stroll among the flower beds, of the many who lie at rest beneath your feet. Across William Brown Street is a fine collection of buildings (somewhat less impressive from the rear than

from the front!). Adjacent is the Liverpool Museum and William Brown Library, boasting a planetarium as well as an aquarium. The circular building is the reading room of the Hornby Library, labelled (or perhaps 'libelled'?) by some long departed humorist, 'Picton's Gasometer'.

Less than polite, perhaps, but we can see where he's coming from.... The analogy was based on the fact that the Victorian building's foundation stone was laid by Sir James Picton. Its real claim to fame is that this was the first building in Liverpool to be lit by electricity.

All roads, it would appear, led to the Pier Head, which was the terminus for many tram and bus routes, and this scene was a familiar one to workers commuting across the water by ferry. Plentiful public transport coupled with the regular ferry service opened up a wider choice of employment to those seeking work. A bus station was to be built in later years.

We would probably be safe in saying that the photograph - dated 2nd May 1936 - shows Liverpool's three most well-known buildings. The famous Liver Birds atop the twin domes of the Royal Liver Building have welcomed travellers arriving in Liverpool since the building was completed in 1911. Alongside it stands the headquarters of the Cunard Steamship Company, built in 1916. Cunard has been a familiar name in the city since Samuel Cunard, a Canadian by birth, established a transatlantic steamer service more than 150 years ago to carry passengers and mail. Note the unusual shape of the building, which is narrower in front than at the back. The third building is the head office of the Mersey Docks and Harbour Company, whose elegant looks and exceptional copper dome caused some controversy when the building opened in 1907.

The Goree Piazzas were built in 1793, in the days when Liverpool was part of the 'slave triangle'

This fascinating gull's eye view captures the essence of the life of the Mersey. The floating roadway, to the left of the Royal Liver Building, is busy with vans and horse-drawn vehicles queuing for the luggage boats, while on the waterfront the floating landing stage is crowded with passengers waiting to board the ferry. The wide white wake on the right edge of the photo-graph shows us that a ferry is just leaving. In the background, note the overhead railway - once so much a part of the city and still sadly missed. Behind the Port of Liverpool building we can pick out the Goree Piazzas, a row of warehouses built in 1793 and named for one of the Cape Verde islands in the days when Liverpool was part of the 'slave triangle'. To its right is Canning Dock. Albert Dock lies empty below, distinguished only by mud. The Liverpool waterfront has changed out of all recog-nition since 1930, when this bustling scene was recorded. The area, however, has not been allowed to die, and ambitious regeneration schemes have in recent years given the city's waterfront a new lease of life.

Left: 'Spot the landmark' is a game we could play with this bird's eye view of the city, which gives us a fascinating glimpse back in time. The photograph is dated 29th September 1932, and wartime bombing and later redevelopment was to make vast changes to our city centre. The sight of the old Lewis's department store, virtually destroyed in the May blitz of 1941, will bring a touch of nostalgia. On the right edge of the photograph, readers will pick out the India Buildings, today housing a modern shopping arcade, with Martins Bank - now Barclays - nearby to its left. It was here that gold bullion was stored during World War II prior to being shipped to Canada and safety in case of Nazi invasion - though at the time any sea voyage was in itself a risky business. St Nicholas' Church - known fondly as the Sailors' Church - is still remembered for its long-ago tragedy: in 1810 the church tower collapsed, and 25 unfortunate worshippers were killed including 17 girls from the Moorfields Charity School. Not too far away is Derby House, where in a fortified basement the Battle of the Atlantic was co-ordinated during World War II. Derby House today houses the Western Approaches Museum.

Above: Towards the top left of this aerial view, Lime Street Station, with the Great Western Hotel alongside, is easily recognised, and the luxurious Adelphi Hotel (immortalised in the late 1990s by the medium of television) is not too far away towards the right. Bombing raids during the second world war flattened whole areas of Liverpool. By 1959, the date of this photograph, the reconstruction of the city was well underway. Before rebuilding began, bomb sites were often flattened and used as car parks in the interim, and some were planted as gardens. The gardens off-centre to the right eventually became the site of the new bus station. Queen Victoria's monument in Derby Square is easily picked out in the bottom left quarter of the picture. Spot the White Star Building in nearby James Street; the design of the building is similar to that of Scotland Yard in London, which was designed by the same architect. The ventilation shaft for the Mersey Tunnel is easily distinguished on the left. Noted for its elegant Art Deco style architecture, the structure echoes ancient Egypt, as does the tunnel entrance, top left of the photograph.

Around the shops

> The twin towers which marked Bunneys' Corner were once a familiar landmark in the city and were demolished in the late 1950s

Through all the changing scenes of life people still have to go shopping - and Bunneys department store was all part of Liverpool's shopping experience. Saturday was the big shopping day, when people would descend on the city centre to browse, to try on, and sometimes to buy. We have no date for this nostalgic shot, but the cars and fashions speak of the 1940s - and as clothes were still rationed until 1949, the options for the shoppers seen here would have been rather limited. The ornate twin towers which marked Bunneys' Corner at the time were once a familiar landmark in the city, part of our heritage which we took for granted, like fresh air, sunshine, and the Liver Birds. But this pleasant and distinctive architecture was in fact doomed. In 1956 the Greenwoods menswear chain took over the store and went on to demolish it. The typical 1960s style of architecture which replaced Bunneys had as much character as your average ball point pen. The building is currently occupied by a shoe shop. Church Street itself has seen many changes since those post war days, and is now one of our traffic-free shopping areas.

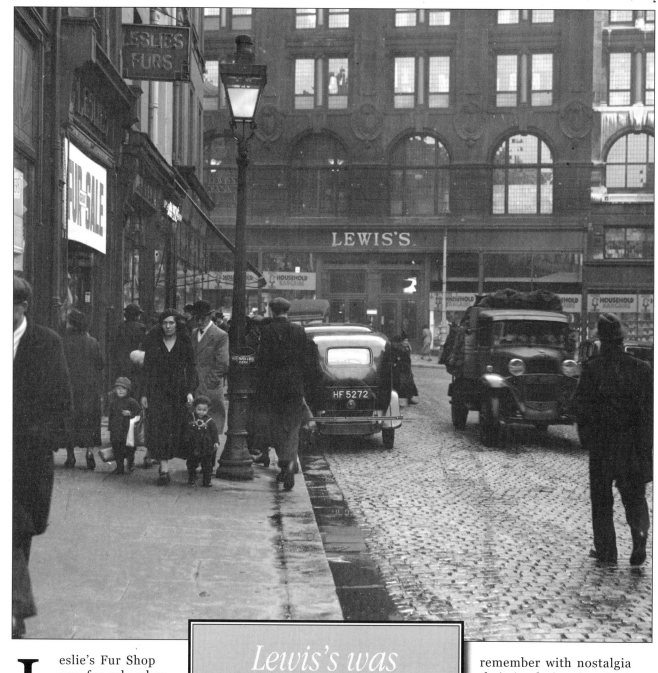

Leslie's Fur Shop was for sale when a photographer recorded this scene in Great Charlotte Street, though this was many years before the tide of public opinion swung violently against the wearing of fur. Fur was very much a fashion statement in 1922, the date of the photograph, and 'genuine' was a description to be proud of rather than embarrassed by. The fact that your collar was genuine fur was often reinforced with the head of the unfortunate animal! But faux was the way to go, and 50 years on lay the heyday of 'fun fur'. Some of our lady readers will no doubt

Lewis's was destroyed when Great Charlotte Street fell victim to the blitz in 1941

remember with nostalgia their 'ocelot' or 'ermine'; those fake furs might have been cheap but they were not 'tacky'. Stylish and affordable, the fun to wear furs could be seen everywhere.

The old Lewis's department store advertises 'Household Bargains' in the background of the photograph. Lewis's is still fondly remembered by Liverpudlians who are old enough to have shopped there before it fell victim to the blitz that devastated Liverpool in May 1941. You may also remember the heartbreaking piles of rubble. Lewis's, however, managed to reopen in part of the building before the end of the war.

Below: Who in Liverpool does not remember Blacklers? The store was sadly missed when it closed in the late 1980s; Weatherspoons now occupies the same place, while H Samuel's next door was to become a fast food burger bar. The neat little hats, the swirling, calf-length skirts, and the vehicles in this shot of Great Charlotte Street all speak of the 1950s. It was in fact 1955 - a decade after the end of World War II - and ladies' fashions reflected the end of wartime rationing of dress materials. For the first time since the days of Edwardian dandies, men's fashions began to hark back to those days of elegance - and Teddy Boy gear was born. Young men adopted velvet-collared jackets with padded shoulders, drainpipe trousers, and crepe-soled shoes which quickly became known as 'beetle crushers'. Cars, too, were changing their 'any colour as long as it's black' image. Mudguards and running boards like those

on the old 'sit up and beg' designs were set to become a thing of the past; headlights would be faired-in and incorporated into sleeker body lines, and flashing indicators would replace the semaphore type. Remember how easy it was to forget them and leave them sticking out?

Bottom: The clock on the corner of Owen Owen - one of Liverpool's favourite department stores - informs us that it is 2.50pm, and a fine, sunny day has brought the shoppers out in full force. The fact that several people are carrying their coats over their arms indicates that the weather is very warm. The photograph is dated 1947, and the wording on the Smith's potato crisps delivery van on the right tells us that they were already accepted as being 'world famous'. The attitude to crisps appears to have been slightly

different at the time; they are described on the cab door as 'The modern table delicacy'. Remember those little blue bags of salt that every packet contained back then? Clayton Square has changed more than a little since the late 1940s. How many readers remember browsing around St John's Market - often a weekly trip? The market was closed in 1964 and in 1986 after a public enquiry the market, together with the surrounding property including the News Theatre, Browns with its beautiful facade, and Littlewoods Cafe, was demolished for major redevelopment.

Clayton Square was originally an area of exclusive housing, named after a 17th Century influential citizen, William Clayton. He was Mayor of Liverpool back in 1689.

A company synonymous with Liverpool

It can safely be said that T J Hughes is the best known name in London Road. Indeed, the company itself, T J Hughes plc, is one of the most famous retailers in Liverpool and a major name in shopping centres and towns throughout England and Wales. Rapidly expanding.

It was perhaps inevitable, from the day he was born on 21st March 1888, that the company's founder, T J Hughes would eventually choose to set up in business as a retailer in his home town, the city of Liverpool. Thomas J Hughes' father, James Hughes came from the Corwen area of North Wales and was also in the retail industry. Consequently Thomas, a Welsh Liverpudlian, grew up surrounded by all aspects of the trade.

The Hughes family dynasty had in fact, originally begun when James married his wife, Anne. Previously, James had worked for Edward Morris and Anne had gathered vital experience working in a shop. Together however, the couple bought their own shop in Old Hall Street and along with this, purchased 11/13 Country Road in Walton. When they opened the shop in 1889, it became the first, though not the most famous, Hughes store.

Thomas was only a year old when his parents opened their first shop and as a result, enjoyed a childhood filled with memorable experiences of life within the retail industry. After leaving school, Thomas served his apprenticeship as a draper at Audley House, then Owen Owen. He must have enjoyed the experience but, little did he know then, that he would end up owning the place and running his own business from there! After completing his apprenticeship, Thomas went to work briefly at Blackler's in Liverpool and then moved to London to work. However, after gathering this invaluable work experience outside the family business, Thomas moved back to Liverpool once again and began working for his father.

Thomas had clear ideas of how a business should be run and was, necessarily, an ambitious and innovative man. Unfortunately, he and his father had contrasting opinions and they often disagreed violently with one another. For the sake of both

Above left: TJ Hughes, during his days in the Royal Flying Corps in the first world war.
Below: A spectacular view of the shop which dates from the 1950s.

men, something had to be done and fortunately, in due time they both agreed on one matter. Thus, in 1912, by mutual agreement, Thomas J Hughes left his father's firm.

On leaving the family concern, Thomas resolved to set up on his own. In the October of the same year, 1912, with the help of his savings which amounted to £150, Thomas J Hughes managed to found his own business and opened a shop at the corner of London Road and Norton Street with the name, T J Hughes above it.

In the early days, the store was comparatively small. However, despite its size, the fledgling business soon began to thrive and it was not long before Thomas himself found that even a small concern could prosper given low profits and a rapid turnover.

The advent of the first world war brought with it a certain amount of disturbance for T J Hughes. It was during these years that Thomas himself temporarily left his business in order to join the Royal Flying

Corps and serve his country. Indeed, this was a brave and admirable decision and, in fact, Thomas' name was added, along with his brother Hugh's, to the European War Roll of Honour compiled by the Calvinistic Methodist Church of Wales. By the time Thomas had to leave for war, he had employed three assistants to help him run T J Hughes. Fortunately, whilst he was away, Thomas left the store in the capable hands of one of his assistants, Miss Harris and it was she who carried on the good work in his absence.

In this way, T J Hughes managed to continue in operation throughout the war and remain intact and ready to resume full trade once again at the end of hostilities. By then, there was also another, separate addition to the Hughes' family dynasty in the shape of the first Babyland shop which was opened by Mrs W Hughes in County Road in the year 1916. Sadly, in 1922, Thomas' father, James Hughes died. This unhappy event also marked another development in the

Above centre: *An early line drawing which depicts the shop as it would have been in the 1920s.*
Below: *The Hughes family. TJ is third from the left.*

> *TJ Hughes was known by everyone as a kindly man who was well liked by his staff*

the corner of London Road and Norton Street were becoming seriously overcrowded. The meeting with Duncan Norman could not have come at a better time. The men agreed that Thomas would sell his business to a small private company to be known as T J Hughes & Co Limited. Thomas would be the sole managing director of the company with Duncan as chairman and the only other director, and this newly formed company would move into part of Audley House with an option to expand further if necessary.

Subsequently, Thomas retained all the company's six per cent preference shares and half the ordinaries, the others being held by Duncan as nominee of Owen Owen Ltd and on October 7th 1927, the reconstituted company opened for business and T J Hughes embarked upon a new era as a discount store.

It was whilst at Audley House that Thomas J Hughes began to gain a reputation for himself. Thomas was known, by everyone who met him, as a kindly man with a positive genius for the drapery trade and he was well liked by all his staff. One former staff member even remembers being sent to the dentist to have a tooth pulled at her employer's expense and then, on another occasion, being told by Thomas to take the day off when she was feeling ill and go on an all expenses paid boat trip to Llandudno with her fiancé in order to recuperate! Thomas also got on exceedingly well with Duncan Norman and would spend an hour or so a day discussing plans with him. On winter Saturdays, whenever Liverpool Football Club were playing at home, Thomas and Duncan would meet in the city and then walk all the way to Anfield to watch the game from a vantage point immediately behind the goalkeeper. Thomas himself was not particularly interested in football but went to the matches partly because he greatly admired Liverpool's full back, 'Parson' Jackson for the moral example he set the rest of his team!

Thomas was a tall, thin man with a habit of rubbing his hands together when pleased. He was an acute observer who missed very little and much of his success

collective Hughes' family dynasty as on James' death, Thomas' brothers, James and Hugh became partners in the firm that Thomas had left in 1912.

T J Hughes flourished after the war and experienced a period of rapid growth. Consequently, the year 1927 proved to be a ground breaking one and marked an important turning point in the history of the company. By this year, the managing director of the business located at Audley House, Duncan Norman, was experiencing difficulties. One of the most urgent problems facing Duncan, as he set out to put his firm, Owen Owen Ltd, back on its feet was the question of what to do with Audley House. The building was an excellent one, modelled on that of Marshall and Snelgrove's in Oxford Street, London, and at that time was officially valued at £194,000. Now it was lying idle however, its value had plummeted and at one point, under pressure from the bank, it was very nearly sold to another firm for a mere £60,000. Thankfully for Thomas that offer was withdrawn and Duncan began making a search for alternative tenants.

After consulting his architect, Aubrey Thomas, Duncan decided to contact another draper in the London Road area. The man in question was Thomas J Hughes. At the time he was approached by Duncan Norman, Thomas' concern was thriving to such an extent that he was employing 200 people and finding it difficult to cope with all the ever increasing business. The extreme success of the business, at a time when its rivals were struggling, meant that the premises at

Above centre: The Roll of Honour in the Calvinistic Methodist Church of Wales with TJ Hughes third down the centre row. Hugh (his brother) is top left.

stemmed from his ability to discover exactly what the customer most wanted and then provide it more cheaply than his competitors. Every morning he would walk past the other big drapery stores and note which were their most popular lines. On reaching Audley House he would rush in and present the list to his staff, asking them to display the popular lines prominently in his own shop but most importantly, at a lower price! Indeed, Thomas' personal motto was, 'Buy dear and sell cheap' - an adage which seems impossible to live by but which, nevertheless he managed to make a reality.

This, however, was not his only talent. Although his buyers carried out preliminary negotiations, Thomas made all the final decisions himself and even drafted his own advertisements for insertion in the Liverpool Echo. He also had a natural flair for fashion and as a result, as well as one of the cheapest shops also had one of the most attractive shops in Liverpool. This success did not come without Thomas' hard work and dedication and it was very rare that he took a holiday but when he did,

he never forgot to telephone his assistants to find out what was happening.

The move to Audley House proved to be extremely successful. Indeed, the two years following the move were ones of unbroken prosperity. It was not long before T J Hughes & Co Ltd took over the whole building and business began to boom at Audley House once again. Thomas' accounting system and some of his organisation was a little primitive, but because people flocked to see the bargains he offered, turnover was enormous. One former customer remembers buying a bed for 19s 11d, two cups, saucers and plates for 1s 6d, and a set of curtain material at 1s a yard - with bargains like these there is no wonder that Thomas was regarded as the pioneer of cut price trade.

> *The two years following the move to Audley House were ones of unbroken prosperity*

Below: *This was the main window of TJ Hughes during the second world war. It shows just exactly how little of everything there was to sell.*

WELFARE FOODS
DISTRIBUTING CENTRE

Above: TJ Hughes' distribution centre for national dried milk in 1955.

Inevitably, after years of almost inhuman dedication and hard work, Thomas began to feel the strains of his success. The pressure he put himself under became unbearable and without a modern book-keeping system he faced a formidable task trying to keep track of everything single-handedly. Consequently, Thomas' health began to suffer. Duncan tried, to no avail, to persuade him to take a

holiday but, although there was nothing seriously wrong with him, Thomas became convinced that he had contracted an incurable illness and that the only solution was complete retirement.

So, on 19th February 1932, Thomas J Hughes finally retired from his business and his post as managing director. His shares were bought at par for £35,000 by Owen Owen Ltd. Sadly, only a year after his retirement, on the 14th April 1933, Thomas J Hughes died in tragic circumstances aged just 43 and although the company still bears his name, this event marked the end of a propitious and unique era. In the year of his death an advertisement was produced for the company promoting its '21 Years Progress'. The advert stated, 'From a tiny shop with three assistants to the present huge store with a separate "Household" building connected by underground subway.

Such progress in 21 years has not been equalled by any other retail store in the North of England!'. Such progress could not have been achieved without Thomas' work, innovation and inspiration.

Despite Thomas' death and departure from the company, the roots had been laid for a stable and consistently successful business. By this time, in order to add to its success, the company had begun conducting promotions outside of Audley House. An existing advertisement from 1935 shows the promotion of the 'Second and Final Week of Furniture Bargains At the Grosvenor Hotel, Rhyl Organised by T J Hughes & Co Ltd.' at which all sorts of furniture was on offer and as the advertisement boasts, all the assistants spoke Welsh and English. Another enterprising promotion from this time was the holding of a 'Crooning & Talent Competition' organised by T J Hughes in conjunction with Gaumont British. To enter the competition, candidates had to make a 6d record at the T J Hughes recording studio either, 'singing, crooning, reciting, mimicking, violin, piano' and the lucky winner was to be sent on a 'free trip to London with a friend - all expenses paid, to visit the Gaumont British Studio at Shepherd's Bush'.

There is no doubt that these promotions played their part in the continued success of the business and at the outbreak of war T J Hughes still held a very healthy position in the market place. However, the advent of the second world war, like the one before it, saw T J Hughes having to adapt to the changes brought by the hostilities and use all of its initiative to proceed successfully on. In fact, it was

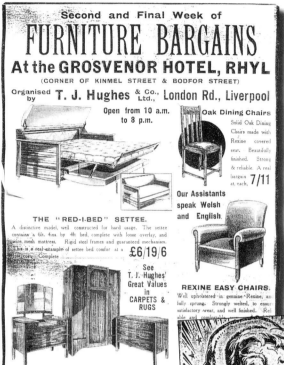

during the war that one of T J Hughes' most inventive window displays was produced. The window displayed two couples, a Mr and Mrs Ready and a Mr and Mrs Unready. The first couple had purchased a shopping bag from the store and so, according to the display 'their shopping bags are conscience free'. The second couple on the other hand, had not been so wise as to buy a shopping bag and so had to carry parcels wrapped in paper, a commodity in short supply during the war! The store also supported the war effort by opening a national savings department for the sale of stamps and certificates.

At the cessation of hostilities, T J Hughes was free once again to accelerate the rate of its development and success. Indeed, the 1950s proved to be a decade of increased prosperity for the firm. Despite this, T J Hughes continued to play its part in aiding the welfare of the nation. In 1955, the store even set aside a space for a Welfare Foods Distributing Centre which stocked dried milk, cod liver oil and orange juice. However, on a lighter note, it was during the mid 1950s that Pinky and Perky and their famous Pop Parade first made a special appearance at the store. The famous television personalities were at the store at Christmas time to assist Father Christmas in providing entertainment for Liverpool's children. The show was a hit and has been followed every succeeding Christmas with ever more impressive decorations, displays and Grottoes including the famous 'Dancing Waters' display in 1961.

The Welsh connection with the store was enthusiastically upheld throughout the following decades. The store's staff wore daffodils on St. David's Day and right

Above: *Two advertisements issued by the company in 1935 and 1959.*

up until the 1960s Thursday was designated Welsh Day, with coaches arriving from North Wales. Up until the 1970s, in order to avoid confusion between the Welsh surnames, only one member of staff with each name was allowed and if a second person with the same surname started they were given another surname starting with the same letter!

The 1970s and 1980s too, were filled with an abundance of consistent success and prosperity for the business. Yet, despite these achievements, these decades paled in comparison to the success of the 1990s. For it was not until 1990 that T J Hughes' rapid expansion programme got underway and the business grew beyond all recognition.

During this time, T J Hughes began to expand its operations by opening new outlets of its Liverpool store. The business grew to such an extent that it was able to become a publicly quoted company on the Stock Exchange and as such, operate under the name, T J Hughes plc. By September 1999, T J Hughes had reported one of its best ever periods for the 26 weeks ending 31 July 1999. The activity during this period mainly consisted of the opening of even more new stores. One of those included the first T J Hughes outlet in the South of England, situated in Eastbourne, which itself created over 100 new jobs. Record results were also documented in this year when the turnover for all the stores

Above: The store in 1961, showing one of the famous Christmas grottos, named 'Dancing Waters'.

increased by 24 per cent to £125.8 million and 'like for like' sales improved by 7.3 per cent. In the September of 1999 the first T J Hughes outlet in Wales situated in Wrexham was opened and proved to be highly successful, as did the opening of another outlet in the north east, Middlesbrough a month later. The beginning of the new millennium has seen stores open in Boscombe, Crawley, Weston Super Mare and Burnley with more planned towards the end of 2000.

Today, over 85 years after the foundation of the first small T J Hughes shop in 1912, the company has risen to new heights. The group now has over 30 outlets and a total workforce of more than 2,500. T J Hughes plc is one of Liverpool's great business success stories and despite its size, continues to function as much an integral part of the city as it was in the early years of the 20th century when Thomas Hughes opened his first draper's shop. Although Thomas would, no doubt, be astounded at the extent of the company's growth today, he would still recognise the same adherence to a proven discount department store formula teamed with the same philosophy of exceptional value for money and very tight operating standards upheld by the company's present Chief Executive, George Foster, that he himself implemented from the very beginning. With the imminent openings of more stores planned for the future in towns throughout the United Kingdom, T J Hughes plc is set to continue securing success at reduced prices for many more years to come!

Left: Tram lines still scored Church Street when this view was snapped back in 1947 - in fact another ten years of service lay ahead of the good old Green Goddesses and Baby Grands. As we study the photograph we form the impression that each of these pedestrians has a sense of purpose. They all appear to be going somewhere rather than merely being out for a stroll around the shops, so we can perhaps assume that this was taken at the beginning or the end of the working day. Note the ground floor windows of the Parker Buildings, which are boarded up; next door is the well-known rainwear chain Kendall's, who have been 'keeping us dry' for many years. Note the ornate frieze which gives Broadbridges' manufacturing opticians' a quaint Tudor touch. Broadbridges were at the time encouraging passers-by to have their sight tested. The NHS came into operation in July 1948; a budget of £1m was given over to opticians' work - rather a 'short sighted' estimate as in fact the cost rose to a staggering £32m, with more than five million pairs of spectacles provided to the general public. Readers may remember the Labour Government's ruling in 1951 which stated that in future, patients should pay part of the costs - causing Aneurin Bevan to resign in protest.

Below: One of Basnett Street's well known stores was the sports shop which was much loved by Liverpool's anglers, golfers and sporting enthusiasts of all persuasions - and the sign mounted on the wall by the doorway was a thing of wonder. Back in the 1950s, children in particular would stop to enjoy the sight of the gilded fish hanging from a giant rod and line - and our readers may well have been among them. However unlikely the young people of today may think it, children really did take pleasure from such simple things back in the days when families were only just beginning to acquire television sets, and video and computer games still lay well in the future! Other shop signs in the street were perhaps not so pleasant, such as the huge pair of spectacles above the opticians, which makes you feel that Big Brother is indeed keeping an eye on you! Classic car enthusiasts will immediately spot the Morris Minor parked at the kerb, interestingly the first all-British car to sell more than one million. Developed by designer Alexander Issigonis, who also gave us the Mini, this tough little car has remained popular and is today attracting quite a following.

Earning a crust

Both pictures: The Meccano factory in Binns Road factory off Edge Lane was one of the major local employers. Situated conveniently on the main road from the town centre, the factory was easy to reach by public transport or by car. How many of our readers remember working on the wonderful little model vehicles and trains? America and France led the way in producing diecast toys around 1914. Frank Hornby introduced tiny diecast toy cars, which he named Dinky, to his range in 1934, and Dinky quickly became a world leader. Interestingly, the Dinky miniature vehicles began life simply as lineside accessories for Hornby's range of model trains, but they gained instant popularity in their own right. Hornby died in 1938. Dinky reigned supreme for many years, but in the 1950s Lesney introduced Matchbox cars, which became a serious rival. A decade on, other competitors such as Corgi (whose cars were made with windows) entered the lucrative field of diecast toys - and it was the beginning of the end for the old Liverpool company. In 1964 Dinky was taken over by Tri-ang, and the site of the former factory was developed as a retail and leisure park. Model car collecting has today become serious stuff, and most adults can remember giving away - or, horror of horrors even throwing out - boxes full of Dinky cars which they or their offspring no longer wanted to hang on to. At today's prices, Dinky cars and Hornby train sets might not have made them rich but would certainly have brought in a few welcome quid. Boxed examples of Dinky cars from the 1950s and '60s can be worth anything between £10 and £50, while the early '0' gauge Princess Elizabeth and the LMS locomotives can bring as much as £2,000!

More than 50 years on, the old wirelesses which emerged from English Electric in the 1940s have become collectors' items

Both pictures: Like any other large city, Liverpool has always had its major employers: the dockyards, of course; Littlewoods, Meccano - and English Electric. Many of our readers will at one time have worked for one or another; will they recognise themselves, perhaps, among these cyclists and motor cyclists eager to get home at the end of a hard day at the English Electric plant in 1950 *(below)?* A hot meal will no doubt be waiting for the men, and after that they could perhaps look forward to a couple of hours with their mates in the 'Dog and Gun': life had its compensations. Pedal power was obviously a favoured method of transport at the time - it is interesting to note the number of bikes in the photograph. A number of buses and trams are also waiting to pick up passengers, but very few employees owned private cars at the time. Some of these workers may well have spent the day checking wireless cases, as these ladies were doing back in 1947 *(right).* More than 50 years on, the old wirelesses which emerged from English Electric in the 1940s have become collectors' items in their own right. Though these small wireless sets are not worth a great deal in monetary terms, they nevertheless reflect the gentler age before television sets changed our lives forever. Although Britain had a television service as early as 1936 (suspended during the second world war), few people could afford to buy them before the mid 1950s.

Both pictures: The workforce at the Meccano factory in Binns Road was largely female, and hundreds of women depended on the production of these die-cast models for employment. Frank Hornby founded the company at the turn of the 20th century, first of all producing the Meccano construction kits which enjoyed a runaway success. The idea began when he made toy cranes for his sons; the inventive young man quickly recognised the potential of his new creation, and he patented Meccano sets in 1901. He bought the Binns Road factory in 1903 for the production of Meccano, and the bolt-together toy was an unrivalled success for 60 years, making him a millionaire. Back in the days before women aspired to entering engineering, Meccano was a 'boy' thing, and male readers will surely remember the 'must have' quality that put the Meccano construction kit at the top of their Christmas present list! Many an engineer or mechanic can trace his interest in nuts and bolts, cranes and winches, all the way back to childhood days, when they received that very first Meccano set. Hornby eventually progressed to making both clockwork and electric trains. He was particularly impressed by German model trains, which were of exceptional quality, and felt that he could achieve the same standards in a range of his own. He felt that a smaller gauge than the German range would prove popular in Britain, and eventually produced the well known '00' - 0.625 inch gauge train sets.

Below: Liverpool has long been noted as a place of 'firsts', and it was in Liverpool that the first public wash house was founded. The facility made the hated wash day so much easier, and the sight of women carrying bundles of washing, tied securely inside a clean curtain or sheet, on their heads was a common one. Long before we all had electric washing machines at home the wash house could offer the women hot and cold running water, hot dryers and even pressing machines. The fact that they could meet friends every week and have a chat in warmth and comfort turned wash day into a day to be looked forward to instead of dreaded.

Right: Every machine was buzzing on the day the machine room at Lybro in Edge Hill was caught on camera in 1959, and these girls were had at work producing the jeans and workwear for which the company was renowned. Denim jeans had already become entrenched as the fashion of the decade - and they were in fact to remain popular right up to the end of the 1990s. Denim jeans were first introduced in the 19th century, when a factory in Nimes in France produced them as heavy duty workwear. Levi Strauss began to make jeans in the late nineteenth century, mostly for gold mining. They added the now-familiar rivets as reinforcements to stop the weight of the gold nuggets tearing the pockets. By 1998 younger people were beginning to turn away from denim, especially as their elders (not to mention a number of prominent political figures!) were still wearing their jeans. Far be it from the average teenager to be seen in public wearing clothes that in any way resembled their parents' - and jeans began to lose their popularity.

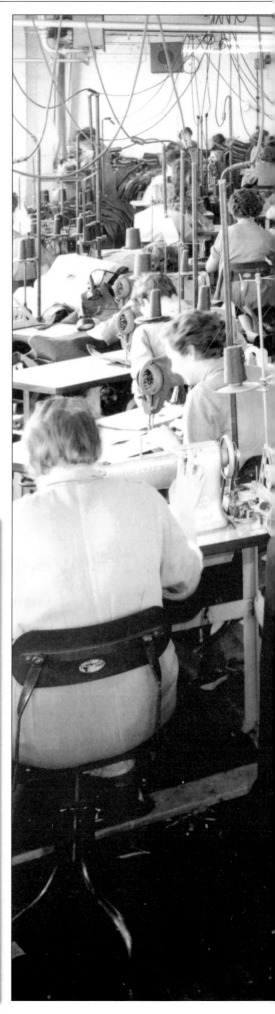

This page and overleaf: As one of Liverpool's principal employers, English Electric did not overlook the social needs of their workforce, and this included Christmas celebrations. The entire factory became a riot of colour as decorations were strung between every available pillar and hung above every workbench *(below)*. Christmas cheer was enlivening the workplace for this group of employees back in 1948.

Every year, English Electric organised a Flower Show, and the event was looked forward to and planned for many weeks in advance. In spite of its title, the Flower Show was not simply about growing and arranging flowers; it was a day out for the entire family. The green fingered among the staff were naturally catered for, but in addition, exhibitions and displays of all kinds and on all subjects were set up within the company's huge canteen. The Show was hugely popular, of course, with people of all ages, but the children came high on the list of priorities. Races and other sporting events were arranged for them, and these became a special feature of the yearly occasion. Some exhibits were more popular among the youngsters than others, and in a straight competition the Hornby Dublo display would come out on top every time *(left)*. A photographer attending the 1954 Show has captured the rapt attention of these youngsters - and that of their parents standing behind! These adults were obviously as enchanted as their offspring at the sight of the miniature trains whizzing around the track, over bridges and under tunnels, stopping at the perfect little stations to pick up their tiny passengers.

BANDS & DANCERS who have appeared at the 'GRAFTON'

FRIDAY May 27th 7 TO 11·30 3/6 Oscar RABIN AND HIS BAND with HARRY DAVIS FEATURING ALL YOUR RADIO FAVOURITES DAVIS. Jack O'HAGAN. BENSTEAD

From previous page: The Grafton Ballroom is the scene of the third photograph, and this happy group of dancers largely consisted of staff from English Electric. What the occasion was we can not be sure after all this time. Perhaps some reader will recognise him- or herself and let us know? This photograph dates from 1949. Ballroom dancing was hugely popular during the 1940s; those were the days, of course, before rock 'n' roll began to overtake it, at least among the younger people, and even if they could not claim to be experts most people could stumble through the waltz, the Gay Gordons, or a quickstep!

The clock in the ferry waiting room bar tells us that it is 5.50pm, and after a hard day's work, what more could a man ask for than a quiet pint, a yarn with the other blokes, and a few minutes' peace and quiet to catch up with the news in the evening paper as he waited for the ferry *(right)?* Note the absence of the fair sex; a visit to the bar on the way home was obviously a male thing! Remember 'Grandad's watch chain'? Our more mature readers will recall the huge chains which tethered the landing stage to the river wall; who was responsible, we wonder, for their strange nickname? The tide was obviously in when the photographer captured the view of the Pier Head *(below)* - the ramps, you may

remember, inclined at a very steep angle when the tide was out. To the left of the photograph a ferry waits for passengers to board; the steam ferry waiting on the right could well be the North Wales ferry which connected with Llandudno. This nostalgic view was shot in 1949. At nearly half a mile long, Liverpool's landing stage was the largest floating landing stage in the world. In the foreground, a closer view of one of the tram circles shows us trams from two eras. On the left is one of our well-loved 'Green Goddesses', while the car on the right is a much earlier tram. The first green cars, which in contrast to the existing cars in the fleet had large number blinds, were introduced to Liverpool in 1933. By the late 1930s many of the older tramcars were showing their age and were given a much needed facelift.

Helping the people of Liverpool get from A - B!

The Merseyside Passenger Transport Authority and Executive have had the responsibility for ferry, train and bus services throughout the area since 1969 with the tunnels coming under their control in 1986. In 1987 the Authority and Executive adopted a new trading name, Merseytravel and still operates today furthering the progress of Merseyside's transport services which, in fact, have an interesting and long established history.

Ferry 'cross the Mersey

It has always been necessary to cross the River Mersey especially at the point between Birkenhead and Liverpool. However, it was not until 1330 that this journey was undertaken by a ferry. The monks at the Priory in Birkenhead received ferry rights in this year from the Crown and took travellers,

Right: During World War II all the ferries contributed to the war effort. The 'Marlowe' helped to load and unload troop ships moored mid-river. ***Below:*** *Even the luggage boat was required to help unload tanks and equipment arriving from the United States of America.*

who had been staying at their lodging house, from the point known as Monks Ferry, across the river in one and a half hours.

The rights of the ferry travelling from the north bank of Wallasey pool were sold separately to the Earl of Chester. This meant that the 'Seccum Ferry' crossed to Birkenhead and from there the Monks Ferry carried passengers to Liverpool. The rights of the ferry passed through many hands but by 1536 the income from

made use of George's Landing Stage. This was followed with the construction of the floating, half a mile long Princess Landing Stage in 1876, and the emergence of the Pier Head area and the Rock ferry's floating terminal in 1899.

By the advent of the first world war several ferries had been added to the fleets. Two of the Wallasey ferries, The Iris and The Daffodil, were commandeered by the government during the war and used as landing craft for the Royal Marines as they attacked the U-boat base at Zeebrugge in 1918. Unfortunately, the ferries were badly damaged but King George V rewarded their service by granting the prefix, Royal to their names.

ferry passengers was estimated to be over £5 per year! Despite this success, it was not all plain sailing. In 1626 a public inquiry was held at which Liverpool boatmen demanded an end to undercutting for passengers. This unrest was calmed but the rivalry and feuding went on until the 1800s. In 1815 the first powered ferry, aptly named Etna, was introduced to the Mersey. One sceptical bystander found this name fitting and commented that 'it would probably explode like Mount Etna' - it did not, and in fact was joined by Vesuvius in 1823!

In 1840, after acquiring the rights, Liverpool Town Council ran its own ferry. Both the Wallasey and Birkenhead Corporations ran services alongside the goods and cargo boats. Seven years later the Council

Two of the Wallasey ferries were also used during the second world war for 'Secret Duty' and sadly, on 8th May, 1941 the Royal Daffodil II was hit and sunk whilst berthed at Seacombe landing stage and took a year to be raised. Fortunately, the only human casualty was a stoker who was blown out of the engine room and consequently, suffered the loss of his false teeth! The Bidston ferry narrowly escaped a bomb and The Bebington and The Oxton escaped unscathed after being used to unload aircraft form cargo and liberty boats.

Top: *The Royal Iris and Royal Daffodil II at Pier Head landing stage, Liverpool.* ***Above left:*** *One of the current fleet of Mersey Ferries, the 'Woodchurch' which arrived on the river in 1960.*

After the war although busy, the fleets were ageing with five Birkenhead boats and six Wallasey boats intact. However, during the 1950s new ferries were added to the fleet. In 1951 The Royal Iris was renamed St Hilary in order to make way for the arrival of the new snub-nosed, twin-screw diesel electric Royal Iris in the same year. The Leasowe was also added to the fleet in this year, followed by Egremont in 1952, and The Royal Daffodil II in 1958.

In 1960 the Woodchurch and the Mountwood arrived and in 1961, after the last journey of the Claughton, finally replaced the earlier steam boats. A year later, these were added to by the Overchurch which was the first all welded construction ferry on the Mersey and in 1963, the last passenger carrying service by a steam ferry was turned out especially to help with the Whitsun rush.

In 1968 the two ferry services were merged for the first time under Merseyside Passenger Transport Executive and Mersey Ferries was born. Indeed, the Merseyside Passenger Transport Authority and Executive became operational a year later and took control of all the Municipal Transport undertakings of Liverpool, Birkenhead and Wallasey. During the 1970s the last new Brighton ferry sailed, the Egremont was withdrawn and the Royal Daffodil II left the Mersey for the Mediterranean.

The Royal Iris on the other hand had helped to launch The Beatles, The Searchers and Gerry and the Pacemakers as well as

Right: *One of the original Westinghouse 'Chicago style' electrics that replaced the steam stock on 3 May 1903.*
Below: *Birkenhead Central Station pictured in 1955.*

carrying distinguished passengers such as the Queen and Prince Phillip. Later, in 1985 she set off on a Merseyside publicity cruise round Lands End, up the River Thames and to Tower Bridge before conducting her last cruise in 1991.

By the mid 1980s commuter passenger numbers had declined and consequently, in 1989, a total of £5 million was invested to re-launch the operation as a heritage and visitor attraction rather than a commuter service. The Heritage cruises proved to be a hit and so the terminals were also improved with added archive and history panels, gift shops, cafes and, at the Seacombe terminal, an aquarium displaying the marine life found in the Mersey. This transformation was rewarded when Mersey Ferries was awarded Visitor Attraction of the Year in 1993, 1996 and 1997 by Mersey Tourism, and the same award was bestowed by the North West Tourist Board in 1998.

Today, Mersey Ferries is continuing to thrive and build upon its long history in order to progress further into the future.

Railway through the Mersey

It was not until 1866 that the Mersey Pneumatic Railway project was launched. By this time the merchants' and industrialists' businesses were prospering on both sides of the River Mersey and as a result, there was a demand for a rail link between Liverpool and Birkenhead. Unfortunately, this project was abandoned as adequate funding could not be found. However, this was not the end of the story as in 1880 Major Samuel Isaac met the entire cost of opening a railway under the Mersey.

In 1881 construction of the tunnel got underway with a toast from the Mayors of Liverpool and Birkenhead. The Mersey Railway was opened on the 20th January 1886 by HRH The Prince Of Wales and in celebration the city's banks closed between 11.30am and 2.30pm and the city's church bells rang out. Indeed, in the Board of Trade Inspectors' report the project was hailed as a 'great and important work'.

Despite this promising start, the initial optimism proved unrealistic and two years later the Mersey Railway was bankrupt. In the meantime, in 1893, the Liverpool Overhead Railway, nicknamed the Dockers' Umbrella because dock workers sheltered under it, was opened. This was the only elevated railway in the country and the first electric railway in the world.

By 1900 the Mersey Railway passenger numbers had gone down from 10 million in 1890 to 8.5 million and the first class stock was no longer maintained. The grime and smoke deterred passengers from using the trains in hot weather and the Company also lost a lot of its passengers to the ferries.

In 1902, the company could not even cover its expenses and its future was put into question. The answer came with electrification which was brought to the company

*Top: Liverpool Central High Level Station at the beginning of the 1970s. **Above:** Commuters arriving at Merseyrail's Kirkby station in the 1980s.*

by George Westinghouse. George owned the British Westinghouse Electric and Manufacturing Company and after coming into contact with Mersey Railway whilst looking for orders, decided to fund the venture himself to the tune of £3,000,000 and guarantee an electrified system in operation within 18 months. The electrification was completed in 1903 and the stations and tunnels were cleaned and installed with electric lighting. The future of the Railway was secured and it began to flourish once again.

Throughout the 1930s the system was enhanced with the electrification of the Wirral section of the LMS company and in 1936, six car trains were introduced in the company's maroon and white colours in order to cope with the increase in passenger numbers.

The advent of the second world war brought with it several obstacles to the continuation of the Mersey Railway's successful progress. Throughout the hostilities half of the company's rolling stock received damage of some kind. Despite this, the railway services remained unaffected and passengers did not experience any disruptions.

The post war period was marked with nationalisation and Mersey Railway was incorporated into the London Midland region of British Railways. It soon became

evident that public transport needed to be improved in order to avoid congestion on the roads. This improvement was achieved in 1962 when proposals were put forward to convert the separate lines and terminals into an integrated system. The Mersey Railways Extension Act received a Royal Assent in 1968 and accordingly, the Mersey Railway was extended to form a loop underneath Liverpool City Centre and connect all four existing routes. A new link was completed connecting the Southport and Ormskirk lines to Liverpool Central and the electrification was extended southwards and northwards. The

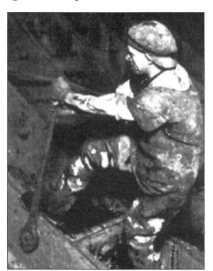

Right: *The back-breaking and labour intensive task of building the tunnel in 1927.* **Below:** *An impressive view of the scale of work undertaken.*

a bridge to improve traffic facilities across the Mersey in 1914. The outbreak of World War I halted any further progress until 1920 when the 'Cross River Traffic Committee' was resurrected. It was renamed 'Merseyside Municipal Co-ordinating Committee' the following year with Sir Archibald Salvidge as Chairman.

The resulting report advised against the construction of a bridge as in the event of war it would prove a target which, if hit, would close the Port of Liverpool. Instead, the report supported the construction of a tunnel and finally, on 8th August 1925, the Royal Assent was granted to a Private Bill authorising the project. The Mersey Tunnel Joint Committee was established and the project was officially underway.

work was all finally completed in 1978 and the Merseyrail Underground was opened by the Queen. Indeed, the system is now Merseyrail.

During the 1980s Merseyrail extended the electrification to Hunts Cross, Rock Ferry and Hooton and during 1985 over 50,000 people used the train to reach the centre of Liverpool. A year later this success was furthered when bus deregulation served to emphasise the reliable and fast Merseyrail system and resulted in an increase in passengers of 12.5 per cent.

Today, the Merseyrail system comprises three closely linked lines: the electrified Wirral and Northern Line and the City Line. With over 45 million passengers using the trains every year, Merseytravel is set to continue expanding and improving rail services in Merseyside for many more years to come.

Tunnel under the Mersey

Although the Mersey Ferries and the Mersey Railway had coped admirably with the transportation of passengers from the Wirral to Liverpool, the cross river transportation of vehicles presented a challenge yet to be tackled. The early Mersey ferries had coped with the volume of horse drawn and early motor traffic but by the 1920s the volume of vehicles had dramatically increased and was still growing.

This problem had actually been recognised in 1825 when the construction of an under-river road tunnel was first proposed. However, the advent of the railway shelved the idea for nearly a century. Liverpool City hosted an inaugural meeting of neighbouring towns to propose the building and financing of either a tunnel or

From a site at the bottom of the dry and disused Georges Dock, on 16th December 1925 Princess Mary (later the Princess Royal) turned a golden key to start the boring machine which initiated the work on the new tunnel - an undertaking which at the time was without parallel in engineering history.

Tunnelling was carried out from both sides of the Mersey and in 1928, the actual breakthrough was made by Sir Archibald Salvidge who sadly died before the tunnel was opened. The occasion was also marked with the shaking of hands through the hole in the dividing

Above left: *The Lord Mayor of Liverpool (Miss Margaret Bevan) and the Mayor of Birkenhead (Alderman F Naylor) shake hands through the hole in the dividing rock in 1928.* ***Below:*** *The Wallasey Portal.*

rock between the Lord Mayor of Liverpool and the Mayor of Birkenhead.

After the excavation of 1,200,000 tons of rock and gravel and the spending £8 million, the Queensway Tunnel was opened to the public by King George V on 18th July 1934. Almost 80,000 people walked through it and the 6d they paid for the privilege went to charity. However at its opening, people were not the only ones allowed to use the tunnel. Tolls were also set for flocks of sheep, herds of cattle, pigs, horses, wagons, handcarts, wheelbarrows and even bathchairs!

After the end of the second world war there was a boom in motoring and local industry and during the 1950s it became evident that a second crossing was needed. After discussions and disagreements about the most appropriate form of crossing it was agreed that another tunnel would be the best option.

In 1965 Royal Assent was given for the Mersey Tunnel Joint Committee to finance and build a second crossing and in 1966 work commenced on the Wallasey Tunnel - later to be named Kingsway. Sandstone was excavated using a giant mechanical 'mole' manufactured in the USA to produce a twin tube tunnel, each tube with two traffic lanes twelve feet wide and just under two miles long. This ambitious project was completed in 1971 and opened by Queen Elizabeth II in the June of that year.

Today, although the growth in traffic anticipated in the 1960s has not materialised, the Mersey Tunnels, because of their geographical locations, continue to play a major role in the Merseyside transport facilities and work well alongside the Mersey Ferries and Merseyrail.

Bus around the Mersey

Electric trams were first introduced to Merseyside in 1898 and the first tram ran from South Castle Street to Dingle. In 1903 the whole system was converted to electrical power. Over the following years the tram system developed into one of the largest systems in the country and was renowned for the amount of reserved track it had in use which served to speed up journey times. However, throughout the 1930s Merseyside's tramways were progressively abandoned and replaced by the bus. This conversion from tram to bus was fully completed by the 1950s.

Since that date the buses provided Liverpool and the surrounding areas with public transport on the roads and worked alongside the ferries and railways. In 1969 the Passenger Transport Authority and Executive took over the responsibility for bus services with a remit to, 'secure the provision of a properly integrated and efficient system of public passenger transport to meet the needs of the area'. In 1974 this work continued with the Merseyside County Council in its statutory role of Passenger Transport Authority.

At the time that the responsibility for the bus services was taken over, there was a total of five

Above: One of Liverpool's famous 'Green Goddess' streamlined trams. Below: The Bus-Rail Interchange at Kirkby Station.

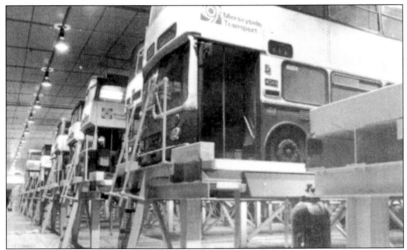

Despite these vast improvements to the bus services in Merseyside, by 1981, there was a marked decline in the number of public transport passengers, partly due to fare increases, unemployment and a rise in car ownership. Therefore, to solve this problem, in 1981 fares were reduced, and this combined with a successful marketing campaign, increased the number of passengers again.

In 1985 the Local Government Act decreed that the Passenger Transport Authority was to be made up of District Council representatives. A year later, in 1986, the Transport Act brought far reaching changes to the bus systems. This Act stated that any bus operator could run any service and charge any fare without subsidy, and that the Passenger Transport Authority and Executive would have no control over the commercial bus services. Consequently, the Executive's bus operations were transferred to a private company.

separate municipal bus operations and the operations of Ribble, Crosville, and Greater Manchester within Merseyside. These services ran to different conditions and in many cases ran in wasteful competition with each other and the local rail services.

The Authority and Executive immediately set to work to develop changes to these outdated patterns and improve the service for the passengers. In order to improve co-ordination, all picking up and setting down restrictions were removed, timetables were co-ordinated and wherever possible, routes were combined. An improved bus service was implemented to reach the suburbs and the trunk bus service was reduced. New services were introduced to new housing areas that were previously neglected and a Merseylink, dial-a-ride bus service for disabled people and those unable to use conventional transport was implemented. These improvements were compounded with a substantial investment in bus operations and the entire fleet was replaced, the average age of vehicles reduced, and improvements were made to garages at Southport and St Helens.

Travel in Merseyside

The Merseyside Passenger Transport Authority and Executive - trading as Merseytravel - was formed to look after all areas of transport in Merseyside and carries forward the progress of transport across, through, under and around the River Mersey. Mersey Ferries, Merseyrail, Mersey Tunnels and the bus services are continuing the proud tradition of first-rate travel originally begun as far back as 1330, helping the people of Liverpool to get from A to B.

Top: *Bickerstaffe Street bus station, St. Helens.*
Above left: *Alfred Road Garage.* **Right:** *One of the fleet of Double deck buses in the early 1980s.*

Gaining ample returns from over 250 years of investment in Liverpool

The Liverpool based company Rathbones ranks as one of the United Kingdom's leading private client investment management groups. However, when it was established the original business was not that of an investment manager but a merchant!

The first known records of the company can be traced back to 1742 and William Rathbone II. In his existing leather-bound Day Book of this year, William's extensive work as a timber merchant is recorded. However, before founding his own business William had, in 1725, moved from Gawsworth to Liverpool to work as a sawyer. During this period in history, Liverpool was a place of opportunities experiencing extraordinary growth. The ambitious William seized these opportunities and it was not long before his timber and ship-building firm was thriving.

The fledgling Rathbone business was run from premises at Duke and Hanover Streets and provided goods to a variety of clients, including cabinet-makers, clock-makers, ship-owners and builders in places such as Wallasey, Sefton and Wavertree. From eight to twelve men were employed at the yard including William's son, William III, who joined the firm in 1745.

Sadly, in 1746 Rathbones' founder died. However, the extensive links he made with his Quaker friends stood the firm in good stead as amongst them Elizabeth Fry and Richard Reynolds the philanthropists, and the banking families Gurney and Tuke all later became business associates. William III therefore, inherited a successful concern and himself took it forward introducing a merchanting business which flourished alongside the timber and ship-building concerns to become world-wide. Timber was purchased for the yard from a network of agents in Amsterdam, Danzig, Barbados and Boston and to fill empty cargo space, other goods such as tallow, iron bars, wheat, sugar, salt, coffee, lead, tobacco, leather and ginger were also sold with 2.5 per cent commission plus shipping charges. However, despite his ambitious nature William refused to make any profit out of the growing slave trade.

In 1768, the firm added several warehouses and buildings to its premises and by then also owned several ships. In 1789 William extended the premises again however, this time the development caused a dispute with the Duke of Bridgewater who alleged that his dock had been damaged in the work. The dispute was not settled until 1792!

Nevertheless, on his death in 1789, William III left a highly regarded successful business to his son, William IV who had already been helping to run the firm for many years. Unlike his father and grandfather, William IV found narrow Quaker doctrines untenable and after publishing 'A Narrative of Events that have lately taken place in Ireland among the Society called Quakers' he was formally disunited from the society - much to his relief! William's liberal and reforming spirit also led

Top: *A drawing of the port of Liverpool in 1728 by Samuel and Nathaniel Buck.* ***Above:*** *William Rathbone IV, 1757-1809, painted by J Allen.*

him to work for the abolition of the slave trade and in turn, to concentrate on trading activities with North America. By the 1800s, the Rathbone business had turned its concentration solely to merchanting and 25, 100 to 300 ton ships with names such as Diana, Kitty, Active and Favorite, sailed to America and Canada, importing American pitch, tar, turpentine, 'new mess in pork barrels and half barrels', barrel staves and rice. It was also at this time that American cotton first made an appearance. Indeed, although not true, Rathbones gained a reputation for being the first firm to import American cotton because the Custom House, who did not know cotton was grown in America, notoriously seized the firm's first importation.

In order to cope with the increased workload William IV had taken on a partner in 1790, his sister's husband, Robert Benson and the firm became known as Rathbone & Benson Merchants. In 1795 another partner, James Cropper, was taken on. However a year later, due to ill health, both partners left and were replaced by William Hughes and William McMurdo Duncan who bought £2000 worth of shares each from Robert Benson. Together in 1801, William IV and William McMurdo Duncan served on the founding committee of the Liverpool American Chamber of Commerce. In contrast, William Hughes did not have

Top: An engraving of Ironbridge Gorge, Coalbrookdale, by James Fittler, published in 1788. The Rathbone family remained trustees and major shareholders in the Bridge until 1950. Left: The statue of William Rathbone V in Sefton Park.

commission work which had become the mainstay of their business.

In 1835 Richard Rathbone retired and was replaced by Edward Dearman. Under his guidance Rathbones was moved up town, away from the river to new premises in Castle Street. Although the period of the 1820s to the 1840s was a time of decline for the cotton consignment business which was strangled by stringent regulations, Rathbones managed to maintain its success. The firm reached a landmark in its history when it became involved in the inauguration of the first regular line of ships sailing to New York. Further work followed and it was not long before Rathbones also ran a regular line of packets to Philadelphia.

The year 1842 was also an important one for Rathbones as William V's two eldest sons, William VI and Samuel joined the firm which at the time had a capital of £40,000. William VI joined as a partner whilst Samuel was not made partner until 1847 along with Thomas K Twist. Samuel and William VI established Rathbone houses at Canton and Shanghai and from there sold British manufactured goods in China and bought tea and silks for export to Britain and later, America. This side of the business was highly profitable. However, due to practical and moral problems the Canton house was closed in 1850 closely followed by the one in Shanghai and from then Rathbones' trading interests in China were run using other firms.

During the mid nineteenth century William VI established the district nursing service as we know it today, with advice sought from Florence Nightingale and in the field of further education he was instrumental in the formation of what is now the Liverpool and Bangor Universities.

such a good relationship with the partners and left the firm in 1809.

Sadly, this was also the year of William IV's death. However, he left a prosperous business and a large fortune including property worth £20,000 to his sons, William V and Richard who were both Oxford graduates. The old partnership of Rathbone, Hughes and Duncan was automatically dissolved but still, William Hughes tried to put obstacles in the way of William V and Richard joining the firm. In the end, Hughes and Duncan continued to trade in the firm's old style and the brothers set up on their own account as commission merchants. Fortunately, the first goods' arrival after this event was consigned to the brother's firm rather than Hughes and Duncan and the Rathbones did not look back.

In 1814, Adam Hodgson joined the business which became Rathbone Hodgson and Co until 1824 when it changed again to Rathbone Bros and Co - the name it retained. Two years before this the Rathbones had assisted in the establishment of Whittaker, Whitehead and Co. William V and Richard's younger brother, Theodore became a partner in this leading brokerage firm and consequently, Rathbones used the firm for the cotton

Throughout the 1840s Rathbones' American trade consisted mainly of importing cotton and breadstuffs to the UK and exporting tea

*Top left: William Rathbone VI MP, 1819-1902, painted by Sir William Richmond RA. **Above**: The Honorary Freedom of Liverpool, granted to William Rathbone VI on 3rd June 1891.*

from China and coffee from Brazil to America. By 1851 however, trade had increased to such an extent that an agency in New York was established to promote Rathbones' business. Henry Gair established the agency and later, in 1854, became a partner in the firm. His position was eventually taken over by William Lidderdale who saw Rathbones become one of the largest China tea importers and in 1864, was also made a partner in the firm and subsequently established Rathbones' London house.

By the 1860s sail was starting to be replaced by steam and Rathbones took advantage of this by joining with Lamport and Holt to build four steamers. In 1864, the fleet of the Liverpool Brazil and River Plate Steamship Navigation Company was formed and Rathbones held the controlling share. The other major development at this time was Rathbones' collaboration with Ross T Smythe in the corn trade. Throughout the 1880s representatives from

Smythes and Rathbones became directors in North Shore Rice and Flour Mills of Liverpool and in 1889 Hugh Rathbone became the last working partner in the business when William VI retired. It was also in this year that the firm's shipping operations came to and end when the Starline steamers were sold to Harrisons of Liverpool.

The 1890s were also years of crisis for Rathbones. The future of the firm was in jeopardy as there was a shortage of merchanting talent in the Rathbone family to replace the previous generation. William VI's son, William Gair VII was a partner in the London house but after his brother, Thomas Ashton's early death, there was no one to take over the Liverpool side of the business. Eventually, Arthur Rudford was appointed this role but, in 1898, the existing partnership was dissolved, the London house was closed and the

Top: *The Rathbone ship 'Scawfell', which made several record voyages between the Far East and England in the mid 1800s.* ***Above:*** *Samuel Greg Rathbone, who joined the family firm in 1842.* ***Right:*** *William Gair Rathbone (VII), William Rathbone (VIII) and William Rathbone (VI) pictured in 1895. All three were associated with Rathbone Bros, over the years 1842 - 1914.*

Liverpool business was re-established on a reduced scale with supervision from the partners of Ross T Smythe. Unfortunately, after its re-establishment the firm's fortunes did not increase. There were losses in the wheat and wool operations and by the 1900s the merchanting business was a shadow of its former self. 1902 and 1903 saw the deaths of William VI and Samuel respectively and Francis Warre (Frank) Rathbone became partner. Arthur Radford and Robert Rathbone were in charge of the Liverpool office and were joined briefly by William VIII who sadly, proved unsuitable for partnership.

By 1912 Arthur and Robert had retired and the restructuring of the firm was completed with a move to modern premises in the Royal Liver Building under Frank's capable leadership. An investment trust started in 1911 brought the business consid-erable profits and it was this, combined with the dedication of Vere Cotton, who became a partner in 1919, that kept the firm afloat during the first world war.

During the inter war years, in 1934, Frank's son Bertram Lyle (Larry) Rathbone joined the firm and five years later, on his father's death, was made partner. The advent of the second world war saw Larry joining the army and leaving Vere in sole charge of the Liverpool office which was in fact, requisitioned. New premises were found at Brunswick Street but this building and all the records in it were destroyed by a bomb in 1941 so Rathbones moved again, this time to Castle Street.

When Larry rejoined the firm after the war, time was spent developing Rathbones' client base. Indeed, this post-war growth included the addition of a total of 500 accounts and the enlargement of the range of private clients and the scope of investment management. In 1949 Rathbones also became

Top left: Francis Warre Rathbone joined the firm in 1902 and remained a partner until his death in 1939.
Above: Eleanor Florence Rathbone, MP, daughter of William Rathbone VI who was concerned with many campaigns for social and political reform.

involved with The Albany Investment Trust and took over the administration of the company. Throughout the 1960s Rathbones established links with the merchant bankers, A Keyser and Co and formed a joint company, Keyser Ullman Rathbone Ltd, which operated for ten years. Vere retired and was succeeded by Larry, Sebastian Rathbone and John Leigh. Overall, this decade was one of success and as a result, Rathbones gained a good reputation for giving advice on capital gains tax.

The firm continued to thrive over the following years. In 1971 Comprehensive Financial Service Limited (now Rathbone Bros plc) was incorporated and this was followed with Larry's retirement from senior partnership in 1979. Sebastian took his place and was joined by the emergence of a string of new partners including Anthony Furse in 1972, Roy Morris in 1983 and Anthony Nottingham in 1987. By 1984 Rathbones had become so successful that its ordinary shares were able to be quoted on the London Stock Exchange.

The year 1988 was a memorable and significant one in the company's history. It was in this year that the Rathbone group expanded through an amalgamation of the investment management and banking business in Liverpool with the international trust and company management and investment management business in London.

The years 1995, 1996 and 1998, were marked with the accom-plishment of further growth. Several firms were acquired including Laurence Keen and Nelson Cobbold, both investment and stockbroking companies, an investment management company in Scotland, and a

> *The 1960s was a decade of success and Rathbones gained a reputation for giving good advice*

trust business in Jersey.

Today, the investment environment is very different from when Rathbones first became a financial institution. The size of the world's stock markets and the number of countries open to foreign investment have increased. Investors now have an abundance of investment opportunities, so the service provided by an efficient and established investment manager has also become increasingly important. This trend has proved to be extremely beneficial to Rathbones, and the Group now offers a discretionary investment management service augmented by banking, tax, trust advice with personal pension management and administration. In addition to Liverpool, the group has its Plc head office in London with further offices in Bristol, Bowness, Chichester, Edinburgh, Isle of Wight, Southampton, Tunbridge Wells and Winchester. Indeed, as one of the UK's leading private client investment management groups Rathbones is in a healthy position in the market place and is set to continue to flourish into its third century of business. The company was recently voted Best Discretionary Portfolio Service and Stockbroker of the Year 1999 by Investors Chronicle readers. In addition it was also awarded winner for "Overall Service Quality" in the latest survey organised by the PAM Guide to Private Asset Managers.

Top: *The retirement party for Vere Cotton (standing 6th from right) in 1960. Larry Rathbone, his successor as senior partner is to Vere's right. Sebastian Rathbone is on the extreme left.* ***Above left:*** *John Leigh, Roy Morris, Sebastian Rathbone, Anthony Nottingham and Anthony Furse, partners of Rathbone Bros. & Co in the late 1980s.* ***Left:*** *The Rathbone flag flying outside the Liverpool office.*

A company keeping in touch with the cutting edge

The Liverpool site has an interesting and varied history and has been at the forefront of telecommunications now for nearly 100 years. Throughout its long history the site has seen many changes and has been run by several different companies. Amongst these have been The Automatic Telephone Manufacturing Company, ATE, Plessey and GPT. Today however, the site is run by Marconi Communications which itself operates as the core business within Marconi plc.

Although Alexander Graham Bell invented the telephone in 1874, it was not until the American Almon B Strowger invented the first automatic exchange that plans were made for the development of the Edge Lane site. In 1903, these plans came to fruition with the foundation of Edge Lane. It was in that founding year that the Helsby Company moved to the site and established The Automatic Telephone Manufacturing Company.

The fledgling company immediately set about working to accomplish its aim by manufacturing Strowger exchanges. As a result, it was not long before it started to reap the rewards of its hard work. Before long the company's small exchanges could be found in operation throughout the length and breadth of the country.

The advent of the first world war brought with it a period of change and adaptation for the company occupying the Edge Lane site. During the war The Automatic Telephone Manufacturing Company turned its efforts to the production of telecoms equipment for the newly formed Royal Flying Corps. Not only that, but the company also managed to find time to provide specifications and drawings for munitions which were produced for the War Ministry and which, moreover, earned a reputation for precision design and engineering.

With the cessation of hostilities the workload carried out at Edge Lane changed once again. However, the success of the operation remained a constant factor, and although The Automatic Telephone Manufacturing Company had got off to a flourishing start this was as

Left: *Almon B Strowger*
Below: *The Edge Lane site in 1912.*

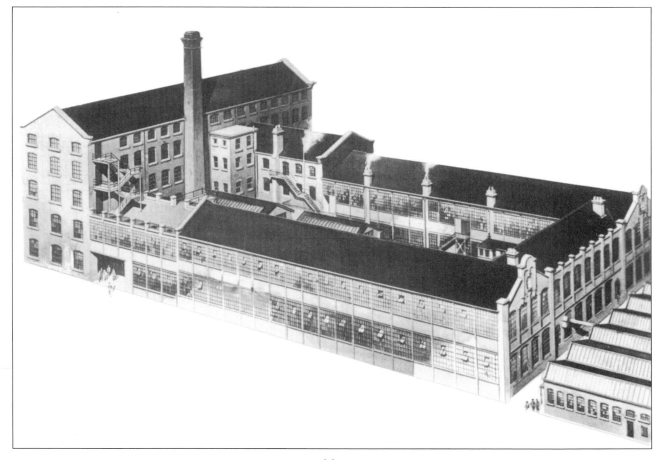

humour of the local workforce was stretched to the limit, but somehow the demands were met. The first 15000-line exchange was installed in Leeds, but it was London where the big successes came. When the company installed the first 7000-line 'Director' exchange at Holborn, Edge Lane was established as a world-leader in telecoms. Indeed, it was Edge Lane technology that created one of the most famous phone numbers of all time - Scotland Yard's Whitehall 1212 at around the time when the newspapers were hailing the birth of the 'Ringing Robots'!

nothing compared to the rate of development experienced throughout the 1920s.

Indeed, the 1920s proved to be a period of exceptional growth in telecommunications, and consequently the company's order books were full and the site continued to expand. This dramatic development did not come without its price. The company's employees found themselves having to work extremely hard all day and every day under the watchful eye of the superintendents in their trilby hats and the foremen in their bowlers who had the power to hire and fire at will! The tolerance and

Despite the recession and the growing shadow of war, innovation at Edge Lane continued unabated throughout the 1930s. It was during this decade that The Automatic Telephone Manufacturing Company introduced the 3000 Series relay to its exchanges. This innovation meant that the company gained a considerable advantage over its competitors as its exchanges were 40 per cent more compact than theirs. Another

*Top: The site is expanding. 1930s. **Above left:** Rack and shelf assembly was vital war work.*

innovative development within the company at this time was the decision not simply to supply exchanges but to add the provision of complete networks, designed by the company's engineers, to its repertoire. Indeed, innovations like this, allied to an increasingly skilled workforce, led to a thriving export market and orders flooded in from Poland, India, Argentina, Manchuria, Australia and South Africa.

The advent of the second world war, like the first, brought with it another period of change and adaptation. This time the emphasis was on sophisticated military communications equipment and, with many men away on active service, for the first time women formed a large percentage of the workforce, initiating a tradition which continues to this day. It was also during this period that A T & T in America developed the crossbar switch. The Automatic Telephone Manufacturing Company was quick to recognise the crossbar's potential and so, when the war was over, work was started on the company's own 5005 version. Remarkably, this version of the crossbar was produced whilst the company was still managing to operate at full capacity in order to meet the worldwide demand for Strowger equipment. Production continued to be very labour-intensive and with virtually every

Right: *HM Queen Elizabeth meeting a member of the staff on her visit to the factory on 18th November 1942.* **Below:** *Strowger and crossbar manufacturing days in the 1950s.*

component hand-made on site, employment at Edge Lane increased significantly and reached a peak at over 14000 workers - half of them travelling to work on bikes!

The post-war decade of the 1950s proved to be yet another period of sustained growth, development and success at the Edge Lane Site. The second world war had highlighted the need for fast and reliable international communications. This realisation necessarily led to an increase in demand for the services provided from Edge Lane. During the 1950s the first transatlantic cable was laid and the majority of telecom manufacturers introduced automated production as well as investing heavily in research and development. Once again, Edge Lane was at the forefront of these developments and in order to cope with its ever increasing workload, The Automatic Telephone Manufacturing Company built a giant assembly shop in order to facilitate the mass production of crossbar exchanges. Interestingly enough, because of its size, this shop was nicknamed the 'Golden Mile'!

The 1960s got off to an eventful start at the Edge Lane site. The early part of the decade saw the successful launch of the magnetic drum, the basis for the register translator. Then, in 1961, The Automatic Telephone Manufacturing Company was acquired by Plessey. Although now part of a much larger organisation, Edge Lane retained its autonomy and became the centre for the design, development and manufacture of Plessey's public switches.

Plessey's reign at the Edge Lane site proved to be a distinguished one. It was under its control that a series of world-beating products and technologies emerged from the site. Amongst these were the first international exchange at Highgate Wood, TXE2, the first all electronic exchange, its successor TXE4A, UHF and VHF data transmission, crystal controlled equipment, and plastic mouldings. All these ground-breaking advances required a large workforce which, at this time, was in excess of 15,000 employees.

During the 1970s, one of the most significant advances of the day was that of computerisation. Computers were becoming an essential part of many industries and

*Top: The 'Golden Mile'. **Above:** Employees leaving the factory in the late 1950s.*

telecoms was no exception. It was at this time that Plessey began providing computerised accounting and billing systems as well as network analysis data. However, despite these impressive advances, the greatest change in telephony since Mr Strowger's invention had yet to happen.

In both Europe and the USA, the race was on to design digital phone networks. In the UK, Germany and France, telephony was a state monopoly and each country viewed the race in terms of national prestige. The British government, therefore, played an active role in the development of the system being designed for the Post Office, called System X. Typically, once again, Edge Lane played a key part in this new development. The government formed a consortium, the major players being Plessey at Edge Lane, and GEC Telecommunications at Coventry who both worked in conjunction with the Post Office's own engineers. In the end the project took eight years to come to fruition and, in 1982, the first System X exchange, built at Edge Lane, was commissioned at Baynard House in London.

After the great successes, advancements and innovations in the previous decades of the history of the Edge Lane site, the 1980s came as a marked and unwelcome contrast. The 1980s was a decade of great upheaval throughout British industry. Traditional working practices were being challenged and the increased automation called for greater investment. The Edge Lane site with its sprawling collection of buildings had served its purpose perfectly in its day when everything was made on site. However, by the 1980s it had proved to be ill-suited to modern assembly methods and, conse-quently, investment in the site had not kept pace with developments in other areas. The workforce plummeted to 5000 and a cloud of uncertainty hung over the site.

Fortunately, the Plessey board had faith in the future of Edge Lane and, consequently, decided to invest £80 million in a seven-year programme of reconstruction of the site. A brand new assembly plant was built; the number of buildings was reduced from 45 to 15; the

Top: TXE4 Rack under test. **Above:** *HM Queen Elizabeth II being shown System X manufacture when she 'opened' the new site on 12th November 1982.*

offices were transformed into light and spacious areas; and the whole site was landscaped. This transformation of the site attracted many high-profile visitors from Europe to see how an old, worn-out factory could be transformed into a centre of excellence, suitably equipped to face the challenges of the future.

It was during the modernisation of the Edge Lane site that two major organisational changes occurred. In 1986 the telecoms interests of GEC and Plessey were merged to form GPT and, just two years later, Plessey was jointly acquired by GEC and Siemens. This meant that GEC owned 60 per cent of GPT whilst Siemens owned 40 per cent. GPT's corporate headquarters were based at Coventry but despite this, once again, Edge Lane took prominence and became the headquarters of the Public Networks Group (PNG) and also of GPT Payphones.

With the completion of the last phase of the £80 million reconstruction programme, it was not long before the Edge Lane site began to reap the rewards of this investment. The site had finally left its cloud of uncertainty behind and had replaced it with a brighter looking future. The Public Networks Group won three Queen's Awards within the space of two years, with an award also going to Payphones. The Edge Lane site itself received its own accolades, winning awards for Best Electronics Factory in the UK as well as Best Factory in the North West. In the meantime the staff at the site helped to win awards for industrial safety, employee development and quality.

In contrast to its uncertain start, the 1980s closed in a rather more successful and optimistic fashion. Edge Lane had been involved in the provision of payphones

since the beginning of the 1980s when Plessey had helped to replace BT's ageing payphones with modern, more secure, reliable and profitable models. By the end of the decade however, the site had become recognised as the design centre for a whole range of coin and cashless payphones, establishing GPT as a world-leader with a customer base in over 60 countries. It was also at the end of the 1980s that, as BT's PSTN network moved towards full digitalisation and as the telecoms market, particularly in the UK, became more liberal, the company based at the Edge Lane site was able to start supplying System X to a host of other network operators, both at home and overseas.

The successful end to the previous decade meant that although the 1990s saw changes as great as in any other decade, Edge Lane continued to flourish. Whilst System X remained a key part of the Edge Lane scene, new technology products such as SDH (Synchronous Digital Hierarchy) were introduced, and are, to this day, helping to ensure the site's continued success.

Today, the Edge Lane site is operated by Marconi Communications, the core business within Marconi plc, which itself has 45000 employees and major design and manufacturing plants throughout the UK, USA, Italy and the world. The assembly plant is still operating at full capacity but, although there are now nearly 3000 staff, only around 500 work on the shop floor, the majority working in the sales and marketing departments. Telecoms has now grown to encompass a global market and the Edge Lane site, from its early days in 1903, has itself grown to meet the demands of this market. Under the Marconi banner, Edge Lane can look forward to the new and exciting challenges always present for a company that succeeds by keeping in touch with the cutting edge of developments in telecommunications.

Top left: *SDH, introduced in the 1990s.*
Below: *The offices - at the start of the new millennium.*

Griffiths & Armour – insuring the right advice

Griffiths & Armour, now one of the UK's leading insurance brokers, was founded in Liverpool over 65 years ago. In the 1930s to succeed in an insurance company required long service and a total willingness to conform. Kenneth Griffiths and George Armour were both in their 20s and wanted to do things their way. So, they resigned their steady and secure jobs and, with a single clerical assistant, put up their plate as Consulting Insurance Brokers.

The gap they had spotted in the market was for impartial client-focused advice on insurance. They saw their role as being to analyse the risks their clients ran and to match those risks with the right insurance. If need be they devised new forms of cover, and appropriate policy wordings, to meet the client's specific needs. The insurance had to fit the client, not the client fit the insurance.

The Liverpool market in the 1930s was still marine-insurance dominated. The city's brokers concentrated on marine risks. Griffiths & Armour was therefore deliberately focused on non-marine risks. It was a bold venture. The partners had no existing business to bring to the fledgling partnership. Their friends were far too young to hold positions of influence and family connections were limited.

They brought to the firm their intelligence, flair, enterprise and professional qualifications but probably above all a great measure of push, cheek and self-confidence. As young men with no family commitments as yet, they could take a risk. Many in the city today will remember Kenneth Griffiths,

Above: Kenneth Griffiths, co-founder of the firm.

who died in 1999, and recognise precisely the qualities he must have possessed in his youth.

The firm took its first offices in the Temple in Dale Street right under the very noses of the partners' former employers. Kenneth Griffiths' father's firm already had offices in the same building and the address looked very impressive on the firm's letterhead. The reality was somewhat different. The premises were already run-down and were to become positively squalid in the post war years when modern office accommodation in blitz-torn Liverpool was like gold dust. Nevertheless the Temple served the young firm well. It was a rabbit warren of small suites and it was usually possible to get a little more space when expansion demanded it. The partners got round the image problem the premises might have caused by a strict policy of either visiting clients at their own premises or meeting them for coffee in the lounge of the Exchange Hotel. It was not until 1967 that the firm was able to acquire more modern offices by acting immediately on the rumour of an impending take-over in the insurance market and securing the promise of offices which would be released as a result. Since 1987 the firm has occupied freehold premises in Water Street.

George Armour was the son of the Rev H S Green of Sandbach, and nephew and adopted son of Theodore Armour, a noted Rodney Street orthopaedic surgeon of his day. Kenneth Griffiths was a scholar of Merchant Taylors' School and son of Ernest Griffiths a consulting engineer noted for his design of the complex building services in hospitals.

George Armour built on his city connections. He was elected to the city council in the year Griffiths & Armour was founded as Conservative Member for Sefton. Within six years he became Chairman of the Passenger Transport Committee and it was under his guidance that the major change from trams to buses took place. He became a JP, an alderman and was Deputy Leader of the Conservative Group on the council at the time of his death in 1957.

Kenneth Griffiths, generally known as KG, meanwhile became well-known as a member and later trustee of the Philomathic Society - a local debating society where the city's barristers sharpened their skills - and of other clubs and societies. He rose to senior rank in the Masonic order. Nationally, he raised the firm's profile within the insurance world through his vigorous involvement in the affairs of the Chartered Insurance Institute. Even in its early years his reputation gained the firm a level of recognition quite out of proportion to its size.

Their enterprise worked. They persuaded a number of well-known names in inter-war Liverpool to entrust their insurance to the new firm. Names from the past now like Philip Son &

Nephew who not only sold books but also produced the school atlas many of us learnt geography from, Chadburns, then a famous manufacturer of marine telegraph equipment and expanding into other engineering activities and Collinsons Cut Soles, now lost to the inroads of synthetic materials into the market for leather soles.

They could not have known it at the time, but perhaps equally important was that they attracted a third partner, James Allen. James Allen was in his early forties and brought with him some important civil engineering contractor clients. This gave the firm the critical mass it needed to survive the war years when new business activity ceased. Most of the staff were drafted into the services and the partners were left to look after the firm's clients, including their war damage claims, with secretarial assistance only. The firm would have disappeared altogether had not all the partners failed services' medical standards, through polio, asthma and diptheria which was then believed to leave inevitable heart problems.

Below: *Dale Street, former home of the firm, pictured here in 1950.*

Happily all the staff returned from the war and a new wave of expansion began; there were more mouths to feed and those who had left for the war as juniors came back as officers and grown men.

The last days of the war saw Griffiths & Armour win an appointment which was to shape the whole future of the firm. It was obvious that following the devastation of the previous five and a half years there would have to be a major effort to

rebuild what German bombs had destroyed. The design professions were gearing themselves up for that effort and the question of professional liability came up. KG's family connection with consulting engineering led to an interview with the secretary and committee of the Association of Consulting Engineers in competition with London brokers. Griffiths & Armour's ideas, innovative as usual, prevailed. But in those days the risk was light - as it remained for another 20 years - and

the income from professional indemnity insurance was minimal. The firm remained, as it had always been, a general insurance broker serving a range of industrial, commercial and construction clients.

The initial importance of the connection with ACE was not on the liability side at all; what it provided was an entrée to a wide range of smallish, but rapidly growing, firms which needed to attract and retain scarce professional staff. One

tool at their disposal was a good pension fund. So the partners researched that market and Griffiths & Armour built up a substantial block of pension business based on the then innovative deposit administration basis which linked the investment return on a pension fund to the insurers' own investment performance - in effect an early

Below: *Water Street in 1952. Water Street is home to the firm today.*

prototype of the unit-linking popular today in many investment products. The partners in the client firms also needed to provide for their own retirements and Griffiths & Armour again seized early on unit-linked schemes, the returns on which have far outstripped those of contemporary conventional policies.

Sadly, George Armour died, whilst still in his 40s, in 1957 and the momentum of the firm slowed. Perhaps it would have done in any event. KG was approaching his 50s and James Allen was already into his 60s. They were ready to enjoy the fruits of their past labours. Having always been characters they allowed their idiosyncrasies full rein. KG was a night owl. He appeared in the office around mid-day, left for lunch and a game of bridge in the Constitutional club and returned to begin his real working day at around tea-time. The staff who assisted him were expected to stay on in the office until he chose to go home. He then read 'the pinks', flimsy pink carbon copies of every letter that had left the office that day. His scrutiny certainly enforced high quality, both of technical content and of English grammar, but it was symptomatic of an almost paranoid need to control all that went on in the firm. There was little scope for initiative on the part of others. Indeed he regarded 'selling' as a dirty word. Griffiths & Armour waited to be asked to advise. Except of course for KG himself! He would sell the firm's services, as opposed to selling insurance, on every possible occasion and with an unparalleled persistence. Perhaps the firm won many accounts merely because the potential client found that the only possible way of escape. Maybe they were happily surprised to find that Griffiths & Armour really did deliver the quality of advice and service which KG promised. Probably a great many of those people and their business are still clients of Griffiths & Armour's today.

James Allen meanwhile had more or less retired from the office for health reasons. The air in Liverpool was very seldom deemed clean enough to permit him to come into town at all. Instead he conducted business from his permanent lunch table at the Prince of Wales hotel in Southport where his clients had regular meetings with him. He must have had great magic, as well as his considerable charm, to persuade them that his services were worth the enormous amount of time these meetings absorbed. Of course the 1950s and

60s were a more leisured age. The entire firm took morning coffee and afternoon tea in Fuller's, along with many others of the insurance fraternity. Perhaps, with a little more enterprise, Fuller's of Liverpool could have rivalled Lloyds of London. Sadly instead it succumbed to the increasing pace of business life and to the automatic coffee-making machine.

The firm provided the partners with a good standard of living and neither of them wanted to share control with new partners. Organic growth continued but there was no long-term planning and no will on the part of the founders to allow control to go out of their families. In James Allen's case he had no children interested in joining the firm. Change only began with the introduction of Brian and Mark Griffiths as partners in the late 1960s, and with a new non-family partner, Derek Pownall, in the early 1970s.

The 1970s were a pivotal era. The Griffiths & Armour of the 1960s and the new Griffiths & Armour which emerged in the 1980s were vastly different animals. The founder partners had aspirations for Griffiths & Armour to continue as a memorial to their effort and enterprise - but no clear strategy as to how the business might be taken forward. The new generation had to develop such a strategy; their future careers and incomes depended on it - but they did not control the firm.

At the same time the firm's business mix was changing dramatically. The clients brought in by James Allen and George Armour were being eroded by take-overs and not replaced with similar commercial and industrial accounts because there were no partners dedicated to that side of the firm's business. On the other hand the firm's professional client base was expanding dramatically. The potential liabilities those clients faced were growing exponentially and their insurance need growing to match the liabilities. The financial services side, acting mainly for the same clients, was also expanding well. These divisions of the business were absorbing trained staff as rapidly as they could be developed, and the firm was reluctant to bring in too many people from outside. The culture of the firm was seen as vital. Griffiths & Armour was and intended to remain strongly client-oriented.

By the end of the 1970s the partnership had expanded and the younger generation was in practical control. Mark Griffiths succeeded his father formally as senior partner in 1984. The first task was to secure what the firm had in an increasingly competitive environment. That involved moving forward a gear from a focus on insurance, but with a strong emphasis on service and claims handling as well as the mere arrangement of cover, to a much more proactive

Above left: *George Armour.*

risk management stance. For the firm's construction profession clients that involved not only a focus on internal risk reduction but equally a major involvement in monitoring and influencing legislative change, the development of industry standard contracts, and in lobbying for change in construction procurement methods. The firm contributes regularly to responses to government white papers, both at UK and EC levels, and advises not only the Association of Consulting Engineers but many other construction institutions, the British Consultants Bureau, the Construction Industry Council, the European Federation of Engineering Consultancy Associations and the International Federation of Consulting Engineers. As long ago as 1972 the firm was asked to help establish a professional indemnity insurance scheme for the South African Association of Consulting Engineers and it now arranges schemes in Ireland, Hong Kong and Turkey, as well as giving advice to similar institutions and clients around the world. The firm has secured its position as a world leader in construction professional indemnity insurance.

Currently the firm is working on expanding its service to the legal profession. When professional indemnity insurance for solicitors in England and Wales became a mandatory monopoly scheme members of the Liverpool Law Society, advised by Griffiths & Armour, voted against the proposal by a seven to one majority. Unfortunately the national vote was seven to one in favour. Some 20 years on the solicitors' insurance fund is having to be wound up and the profession is left to fund hundreds of millions of pounds of under-provision for past claims. Griffiths & Armour intends to rebuild its past involvement with solicitors now that they are once again free to make their own insurance arrangements.

The firm has continued to build its financial services wing, now a separate company in the group, Griffiths & Armour Financial Services.

It has also rebuilt and continues to expand its commercial and industrial account where it aims to become the natural first choice broker for

major north-western businesses. Already it has attracted key people from other brokers. Most other major brokers are either quoted on the stock exchange or owned by organisations whose philosophy is to retain their investment only for a relatively short time and for a quick profit. Griffiths & Armour by contrast remains wholly owned by current and former partners. As such it has no need to satisfy the short term requirements of stock market analysts. Its main focus is on its service to clients rather than on the bottom line. That is as attractive to people who wish to give a first-class service as it is to clients who seek that standard of service.

Griffiths & Armour is proud to be a Merseyside business which owns a Lloyds broker. Too often the ownership of most important businesses is focused in London. The firm has expanded its operations not only into London but also into Glasgow, Dublin and Hong Kong and, through joint ventures, into South Africa and Turkey as well as running specialist captive insurance facilities in Guernsey.

Griffiths & Armour is now a household name. It is a strong invisible exporter for Liverpool employing Merseysiders and feeding local insurance markets. When the city council claimed to be 'fighting for jobs' Griffiths & Armour was actually generating real employment in spite of the handicap of the 'loony left' image which Liverpool's local government seemed to glory in. Griffiths & Armour has come through that era and emerged as a serious and major broker not only on the national stage but internationally as well. With Liverpool's improving image Griffiths & Armour intends to remain true to its roots and to be as important on its own territory as it is on a wider stage.

The creation of two egocentric and opinionated young men has come a long way - really it has been the creation of all those who have contributed to the firm's growth and development over 65 years, and if the commitment of present and future partners and staff matches that of their predecessors, Griffiths & Armour still has a long run before it as a standard bearer for Merseyside.

A fruitful history worth preserving

The Liverpool based preserving company, Nelsons of Aintree has been producing jams and preserves from choice selected fruit and the finest sugar for over 75 years. It was in fact, in the year 1921 that the Nelson Preserving Company was established and first began in production.

However, it was perhaps not immediately inevitable that when the company's founder, Tom Porter decided to set up in business he would choose to establish a preserving company. His enterprising and entrepreneurial spirit was, nevertheless apparent from the start. Indeed, after leaving school at the age of 14, Tom became involved in a totally different kind of business to food production. He began his working life wholeheartedly, and without any help actually founded, set up and ran a saddlers! This business proved to be successful. However, the advent of motor transport put a stop to the further growth and development of the saddlers. Motor transport largely replaced the horse and when, as a result, the trade in saddles inevitably declined, Tom was quick to adapt.

He tapped into the reserves of his enterprising spirit once again and decided that the jam industry would become his future trade. In the early part of the 20th century, particularly in the years leading up to the advent of the first world war, the British were great jam eaters. Consequently, the production of jam made up a substantial percentage of the food industry as a whole - Tom had chosen wisely.

Tom's first step into the jam industry could more aptly be described as a giant leap. Initially, Tom began by setting up another company which he called Porters' Perfect Preserves. However, this soon evolved into The Nelson Preserving Company which he established in 1921. Tom started his new business venture from a site located at Long Lane in Aintree, Liverpool and indeed, the company remains at the same site to this day. A purpose built factory was constructed on the site which was equipped to cope with the handling of

Above: Two of Nelson's early jar labels.
Below: Labour intensive jam making in the 1930s.

company also used a significant amount of strawberries and raspberries imported from Eastern Europe.

In the early days of the history of the business, manufacturing methods were quite basic and extremely labour intensive especially so when compared with today's processes. The ingredients were hand loaded into large copper pans with pouring spouts. Once full, the fruit was boiled and when the jam was ready, the pans were tilted by operatives until the jam had filled all the necessary containers. The jam was poured into bottles by hand and the bottles were then held in open wire cages and stacked and cooled overnight. The final part of the process involved the operatives having to complete the

all the different types of fruit associated with preserves and it was from there that the first Nelson's jams were produced. Many of the different types of fruit were sourced in the United Kingdom. However, it was not long before the company started to import fruit. Amongst the imported fruit were apricots as well as bitter oranges from Spain which were used in the production of marmalade. The

packaging of the jam with the use of lids, labels and boxes. The handling of the fruit was also very basic. It was packed in large wooden casks and in this way, large stocks of fruit were stored all the year round for

Top: The canning room pictured during the 1930s.
Above: During the 1950s increased automation made the process of jam cooling and sealing much easier.

use between seasons. The use of the wooden casks meant that coopers had to be employed by Nelson's in order to check the barrels and maintain the tension of the hoops around the wooden staves, ensuring that the fruit did not get damaged.

As the business developed, in common with all industries, automation eventually began to make things easier. Automatic filling machines were introduced for filling glass jars and cans. Later, cooling equipment was introduced which worked by spraying the lidded jars with water, and as well as this, labelling equipment was installed.

Tom's fledgling business continued to flourish. The inter war years proved to be ones of success and development. It was during these years that Nelson's won one of its most important contracts bringing increased levels of prosperity to the company. This contract came from Woolworths. Nelson's supplied jams to them under the Crystal Gold label, indeed, for many years Woolworth's was Nelson's best customer. However, the other products that took up a major part of the production at the time, were 7 lb. tins of jam.

The advent of the second world war brought with it several changes to the running of Nelson's. The company, like many others at the time, did experience the problem of shortages. Not only was sugar rationing in force and an obstacle to the company's success but also other supplies were lost at sea. However, unlike some other companies, fortunately Nelson's managed to continue trading. During wartime Nelson's had a contract with the Ministry of War which involved the company with supplying its preserves to the armed forces and in part, it was this that helped to keep Nelson's up and running.

After the war, the business remained a successful concern and in fact, blossomed into a truly family run firm. The founder's sons, John and William joined the business and both went on to play an important role in the progression of the company.

Top: *Modernised building for bakery jam production.*
Above right: *Bakery jam filling room.*

The year 1965 was an important one in the history of The Nelson Preserving Company. It was in this year that, in order to further develop the business, the company was sold to the Associated British Foods Group. The Associated British Foods Group retained all the Nelson staff and the increased investment in the firm led to increased sales of Nelson products. Indeed, to this day Nelson's remains a part of the Group and as a result, is still recouping the benefits of the substantial investment from its parent company.

The decade of the 1970s brought with it yet more changes and advancements in the development of the company. During the early part of the decade the company made a conscious and positive decision to seek more of its trade overseas. This led to the development of very high quality preserves made from the very best raw materials and products which would suffice to satisfy the stringent requirements of countries such as the United States, Europe and the Far East.

The process of investment in luxury products and the export trade continued, and in fact was accelerated and further developed during the 1980s.

In the year 1996, the Nelson Preserving Company reached its 75th year in business and, due to the healthy position of the business at the time, was able to celebrate its anniversary in style. A year after its 75th anniversary, the company invested in yet more of the very latest, most up to date, jam making technology. This enabled Nelson's to vacuum cook in 2.5 tonne batches with the use of modern jam making equipment with automatic controls.

Today, Nelson's of Aintree continues to operate as a successful concern. The company's equipment continues to feature the very modern technology in which Nelson's have invested including the automated loading of ingredients, automatic process controls, automatic filling and packing lines and continuous quality monitoring. The company's main customers in the United Kingdom now include the major supermarkets, the independent trade specialist houses and the bakers and biscuit manufacturers. To add to this, the export side of the business remains strong, with an export volume that now accounts for 14 per cent of the company's business. The company's markets remain very much as they have always been, consisting of the sweet spread market for jams, marmalades and mincemeat. The supply of bulk product to biscuit and bakery manufacturers has grown considerably and the supply of condiments is a new area which is now a very important part of the business. Nelson's of Aintree provides secure employment for over 150 local people. Indeed, by preserving its fruitful history whilst adapting to meet the needs of today's market, the company is set to continue successfully in Liverpool for many more years to come.

Left: Traditional jam pans, with automated controls.
Above left: The Vacuum Cooking plant.

A centre of excellence at the forefront of research for over 100 years

The story of the foundation of the Liverpool School of Tropical Medicine, as it is known today, can be traced back to its origins in the late 1800s and more specifically to Alfred Lewis Jones.

Alfred Lewis Jones was the Head of Elder Dempster Shipping Line which, under a different name, had initiated Liverpool's steamship service and transformed Liverpool's port into a thriving concern. This transformation brought with it a dramatic increase of trade and, in turn, a rise in the number of patients suffering from 'tropical' diseases such as malaria. Alfred recognised the threat this posed to his workforce and so, when asked to fund the foundation of a school which would conduct research into 'tropical' diseases he agreed.

With Arthur's financial backing the Liverpool School of Tropical Diseases was officially opened in 1899 by Lord Lister, the inventor of antiseptic surgery and the President of the Royal Society, at a reception in the Royal Southern Hospital. At this time the new School

was the first institution in the world to be dedicated to research and teaching in tropical medicine and parasitology and as such, began as it meant to go on, pioneering new ground.

The Samuel Henry Thompson-Yates Ward at the Royal Southern Hospital became the site of the first teaching at the School in the May of its founding year. Most of the School's students were qualified medical personnel and those passing the examinations were awarded a Certificate of Tropical Diseases. Professor (later Sir) Rubert Boyce was appointed the School's first Dean.

Right: *Rubert Boyce (left of the man in the top hat) in Barbados in 1909, during the School's 22nd expedition.*
Below: *Staff and students outside the Johnston Building in 1912.*

Subsequently, he selected the School's first salaried member of staff, H E Annett as a demonstrator in Tropical Pathology, followed by Major (later Sir) Ronald Ross as a lecturer in Tropical Diseases.

In fact, it was Ronald Ross who conducted the School's first scientific expedition to Sierra Leone to study malaria. During this expedition, with the help of an army of local people, the malaria-carrying mosquito was pursued and its elimination was initiated. Ross' work on malaria was rewarded when he became the first Briton to be awarded the Nobel Prize for medicine.

It was not long before the fledgling School began to flourish. Luckily, philanthropy was fashionable at the time and the School was able to progress and develop largely due to a number of private donations. One of the more influential benefactors was Mary Kingsley the successful author of 'Travels in West Africa' who was also considered an expert on African culture and politics

in government circles. Three years after her death in 1903, a Mary Kingsley Medal was established in her honour, to be awarded for outstanding contributions in the field of tropical medicine.

The year 1903 was also marked with the setting up of Tropical Veterinary Medicine as a separate discipline. Rubert Boyce and four of his friends also guaranteed the salary of a Professor of Veterinary Medicine for five years and in addition, a laboratory was installed in part of Crofton Lodge in Runcorn which made the research of large animals possible. Wolferstan Thomas was appointed as Director in order to carry on at home the work of Dr J E Dutton on African sleeping sickness following the expedition to The Gambia and Senegal on which it was first demonstrated that the sleeping sickness parasite was in human blood. Indeed, it was Wolferstan Thomas's initial research at the laboratory which led to the development of atoxyl as the first effective treatment for sleeping sickness and his colleague, Anton Breinl who contracted the illness and was treated with his own drug!

From its inception the Liverpool School of Tropical Diseases was involved in undertaking overseas expeditions. In the School's initial 15 years, 32 expeditions were completed, mainly to Africa but also to Central and South America and reports of the findings were published in the School's Memoirs and Annals. During

Top: A laboratory at the School at Crofton Lodge, Runcorn. *Inset:* The exterior of Crofton Lodge. *Above:* Nursing staff on the roof of the Tropical School Auxiliary Military Hospital.

Whilst time was spent restoring normality at the School after the war, a permanent base was also being developed in Africa. With the use of some of Alfred Jones's bequest, a research laboratory was set up in Freetown, Sierra Leone. The Laboratory was completed in 1921 and work was initiated, at first concentrating on the West Coast of Africa. This work provoked some important findings, including the discovery that blackfly can transmit the worm that causes river blindness in Africa and parts of Latin America and, that a local species of snail was implicated in the transmission of schistosomiasis. The Laboratory also participated in an emergency yellow fever vaccination programme in The Gambia and The Bathurst Drainage Scheme and in this way furthered the School's commitment to local affairs.

an expedition to the Congo Free State in 1904, Dutton and Todd discovered the transmission of 'tick-fever' and provided material which marked the beginning of research into the type of parasites causing the disease in humans. Sadly, Dutton died of the disease in the Congo in 1905 and a year later the causative agent was named, Borrelia Duttoni in his honour. Research was also undertaken into yellow fever and the School founded a Yellow Fever Laboratory in Manaos but the project was beset by financial problems and ended on Wolferstan Thomas's death in 1931.

The School's financial position was greatly strengthened when, on his death, Alfred Lewis Jones left several large bequests in his will to the institution he had helped to set up in 1898. As a result of this donation, the School was able to erect its own Laboratory separate from the University which formed the basis of the main building in Pembroke Place. The construction of the laboratory was completed in 1914. However, this proved to be rather bad timing and the advent of the first world war meant that the School's occupation of the building had to be deferred. In the meantime, the building did not stand idle and, in fact, was used as a Tropical Diseases Hospital and short courses for officers of the Royal Army Medical Corps were provided by the staff.

Dr (later Professor) R M Gordon joined the School in 1919 and a year later, in 1920, was able, along with the other staff, to make use of Pembroke Place and from there the teaching and research was resumed. As well as the lecture rooms, research laboratories and insectary, a museum was also established at the premises. This evolved into an important teaching aid and even won awards for its exhibits before it was dismantled in 1937.

Unfortunately, during the 1930s it became difficult to find funds for the Sir Alfred Lewis Laboratory. Consequently, the School had to take over the supervision and training of the Pathology staff. Despite this, with the advent of the second world war, the workload of the Laboratory increased. The Royal Army Corps consulted the Laboratory to train its staff in Freetown's Imperial Garrison and by 1940 the workforce of two had

Top left: Dr Alwen Evans, a world authority on malaria, using a binocular microscope near a water-lettuce swamp in Sierra leone. Top right: Dr Alwen Evans at Entebbe Airport, Uganda in 1936. Right: An aerial view of Pembroke Place in 1930.

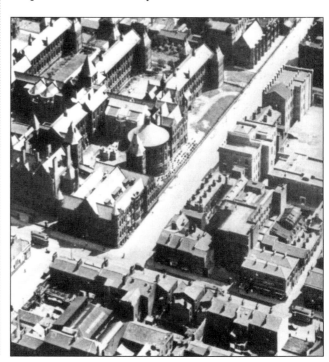

the world which proved to be more severe in the tropics.

As a result of this important realisation, during the decades of the 1980s and 1990s the School diverted much of its attention to research on major diseases amongst children in the tropics. In 1982, using funds from the Wolfson Foundation, the disclipine of Molecular Biology was introduced in the School. In 1998 the School celebrated its 100th anniversary. To commemorate the occasion, with the support of Her Royal Highness the Princess Royal, the School held a Centenary Appeal to raise funds for, amongst other things, the implementation of the latest information technology systems and the development of the Donald Mason Library. After the Centenary the School continued its work in developing new areas of knowledge, including Molecular Epidemiology and DNA vaccines. Indeed, as a testimony to all of its valuable work the School received the Freedom of the City of Liverpool in 1998.

The Liverpool School of Tropical Medicine continues to remain at the forefront of research and health promotion through understanding, education and partnership with the international community. It has come a long way since its foundation with now over 165 members of staff and over 500 students. The School is a registered charity, linked to health ministries, universities and research institutions world-wide and is one of the few postgraduate centres of excellence in the world in the field of tropical medicine. Indeed, with further support, the School aims to continue its ground breaking work for the foreseeable future.

Top left: Pembroke Place in 1975. Top right: HRH Princess Anne, Patron of the School, pictured on a visit in 1985.

to cope with 10,000 army, 10,000 navy and hundreds of naval air force personnel! Finally, after the war when the Laboratory was undertaking all routine government pathology in Sierra Leone, it was realised that the situation was impossible to maintain and the Laboratory was closed.

The School, too felt the effects of the second world war. It helped to train personnel and successfully completed the research of anti-malarial drugs. The School also staffed a temporary Tropical Centre, set up at Sefton General Hospital, and undertook the first British trials of penicillin for the treatment of syphilis.

At the cessation of hostilities, in 1945, Brian Maegraith was appointed Professor of Tropical Medicine. The years following his appointment were spent setting up new departments to emphasise the tropical and international dimension of the work. Indeed, courses were established in Nigeria, Ghana, and South East Asia. Links were also made with the Faculty of Tropical Medicine in Bangkok and the School's extensive list of discoveries and firsts continued.

In 1973, Professor Ralph Hendrickse founded the Department of Tropical Paediatrics set up to deal with the questions around child and maternal health. Consequently, it was realised that the most important threat to health in the developing world was not specifically 'tropical' diseases but those prevalent throughout

Transmitting a first class reputation world wide

The Liverpool based company, MPE Limited has accumulated 75 years of experience in the design, development and production of high performance radio frequency interference filters and custom capacitors for commercial, professional and defence applications. Today, the company is one of Europe's leading filter specialists. However, the innovation that secured this reputation was, in fact, initiated in the early 1900s by William Dubilier.

Born in New York in 1888, William developed his interest in all things electrical in his childhood and had invented an electric shock burglar alarm by the age of 10! In 1905 he studied at the Cooper Institute whilst working for the American Telephone and Telegraph Company. Little did he realise then that the Institute would later award him the Ganc Dunn

Medal for scientific achievements and their citation for Professional Achievement. After qualifying as an electrical engineer, William applied for the first of some 600 patents he was to hold! But 1909 was to prove the year of his real breakthrough. He set up an experimental wireless transmitter at the Alaska Yukon Exposition and his resulting transmissions caused a sensation hailing him as the first broadcaster.

This breakthrough led to work throughout the world and in 1911 William was invited to the UK for what turned out to be a clandestine meeting with the War Office, 'Wireless' Committee. William was asked to assist the government in finding a substitute for the German-made Leyden Jar and in 1912, he produced

Below: *Staff on the assembly line.*

In 1926/7 Dubilier Condenser Limited was chosen to install its power mica capacitors to provide the main oscillator condenser bank at the largest transmitting station in the world. It was also in 1926 that the company's "Cat-Whisker" wireless receivers were replaced by battery sets and the possibility of world-wide communication by short-waves opened up new fields of set design. Indeed, by 1929 the company had six designs in production in its carpentry shop including the first combined radio-gramophone cases.

By 1931 the company had to choose between the manufacture of components or sets. Due its innovative staff, the decision was made to concentrate on components. A year later, through the good offices of William Dubilier, a long term licensing agreement was signed with the International Resistance Company of Philadelphia for the large scale manufacture of carbon composition resistors. This was not the only achievement of this year, it was also in 1932 that electrolytic capacitors were produced with a licence from William Dubilier's Radio Patents Corporation.

a more efficient product, the first modern power capacitor using a mica condenser. Thus, the Dubilier Electrical Syndicate Limited was formed and began production from a garage in London.

By the advent of the first world war the mica capacitor had replaced the Leyden Jar and throughout the war William was free to work on other inventions such as an airborne wireless communication system and a submarine detector. In 1917 however, William returned to the USA to set up his own company. The co-founder of the UK company, WH Goodman continued as managing director and in 1918 new capital was raised to enable the business to become Dubilier Condenser Co Ltd.

In 1925 the firm was restructured and the company that still exists today, under a different name, was founded as Dubilier Condenser (1925) Limited. The post war years were difficult times for the company which had to rely on its mica condenser and portable x-ray equipment. However, the wireless component industry soon established and consequently, Dubilier Condenser Limited began manufacturing condensers, resistors, toroid coils and other related products.

Dubilier Condenser Limited's premises were used by several other firms. Amongst these were Isenthal and Co Limited which produced x-ray appliances and radioactive materials, and Mansbridge which produced capacitors. During the 1930s both firms were taken over by Dubiliers. In 1936, further expansion was also achieved with the building of larger premises in Acton to accommodate extra departments in planning, production and material control, and part of the factory was allocated to a new mineral oil impregnation plant. Although the company also began using ceramic dielectric capacitors at this time it did not produce them and therefore was at a disadvantage having to use outside suppliers.

Top left: *A Reynolds Boughton two ton truck at the MPE factory for suppression.*

Sensible preparations were made for war and wherever possible alternative British suppliers were found to replace those in India, Germany and Switzerland. During the second world war, the company made a large contribution to the government's research work and produced 280 massive high voltage capacitors for protection of the launching equipment of barrage balloons. Due to its important work, the business was designated 1A Priority (Navy) and its order book expanded with more government contracts. The Acton site saw much enemy action and additional duties included the Company Fire Brigade, a Home Guard unit, and a rota of fire watches. Despite this, the site was hit in 1941, demolishing the electrolytic shop. Temporary satellite sites were established and the company managed to manufacture Pulse Forming Networks for radar transmitters.

After the cessation of hostilities, the Acton plant was rebuilt and the production in the satellite factories was transferred to new premises at Kirkby in Liverpool situated on a former MoD site from which some Dubilier employees had worked during the war. During the post war years the company achieved several firsts including the development of new and pioneering equipment, machinery and testing facilities. These innovations were added to when an engineer, R Davidson, joined the company in 1947 and developed new high frequency uses of capacitors, new radio interference devices and much more.

The 1950s proved to be a decade filled with success. A generator was installed at the factory to cover the production in the event of power cuts and a range of components were made widening the company's range. In 1958 a new building on the Acton site provided centralised lab facilities and a key patent was secured. In 1959 the company went into full production of moulded paper and mixed paper and film capacitors. Indeed, over 150 million were made in this initial year.

During the 1960s the company began carrying out approval tests for the MoD and the BSI and itself became one of the first firms to become BSI approved. In 1965 a second factory was built in Kirkby and electrolytic production was transferred to the site which, after losses, was closed three years later. In the space left in Acton a new computer grade resistor was introduced and in 1967, with the rise of a colour TV service, the company experienced an increased demand for its components for receivers. To cope with this demand the Dubilier Component Distribution Operation was formed and sustained the company throughout the following few years until the decision was taken in 1971 to manufacture its own product.

The year 1970 was a tragic one for the company in which three of its directors died and one retired

Below: *HRH Duke of Kent meeting MPE staff at a trade fair.*

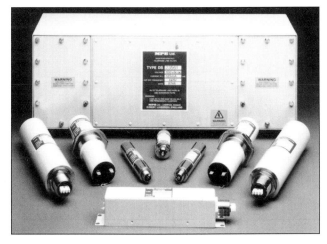

through illness. This left only R Davidson and, with profits falling since 1965, the company was ripe for a take-over. In 1972 this eventuality transpired and MIT Securities took over Dubiliers and in the same year acquired two other company's, Kenneth and Beswick Limited and Greenpar Limited of Harlow.

Under the new management the Acton site was sold, production moved to Kirkby and a new factory was set up at Bootle, Merseyside. Also, Dubilier Components Limited was formed at Bicester to distribute electronic components from the parent company. The company's concentration now focused on special capacitors and radio suppression devices.

In 1981 the company was taken over again, this time by MPE and reformed as MPE - Dubilier until the Dubilier name was finally dropped in 1984. Importantly, in 1985 a Cad System was installed at the Kirkby offices which accelerated product development and met the demand for communication

systems capable of operating in a nuclear theatre and a year later the promising company was bought by the Adwest Group.

Throughout the 1990s the company's portfolio broadened to encompass the Telecommunications sector as well as defence and a wide range of computer-aided capacitor and filter design techniques were used to ensure the efficient use of design resources. In 1997 the firm came full circle and was bought by MPE Management again with the help of the Merseyside Special Investment Fund. Over 90 jobs were safeguarded and under the MD, Peter Cotterill and the Technical Director, Jan Nalborczyk the company began to flourish again. A 100K order was completed for the Middle East including the biggest High Performance Installation Filter in the range. This success was marked in 1999 with the introduction of a new company logo and in the year 2000 MPE Limited celebrated the company's 75th anniversary with the knowledge that every year since the buyout had seen a profit.

Today, MPE Limited is situated at Knowsley Industrial Park and as well as being a leading supplier to the UK defence industry has a rapidly expanding export market supplying major telecom companies. Indeed, the company is a major local employer and with over 100 man years of design engineering experience is set to continue from Liverpool, transmitting a first class reputation world-wide and celebrating many more successful anniversaries.

Top: MPE's Liverpool offices. Top Left: MPE has developed a new modular range of telephone and data line filters.

Staying afloat for over 200 years

The Liverpool company, Bahr Behrend was established over 200 years ago in 1793, and since then has been offering a wide range of transport services to meet the needs of shipowners, importers and exporters.

The company's founder, Lorentz Hansen was born on the island of Bornholm in 1760 but moved to Liverpool to set up as a shipbroker. It was whilst in Liverpool that Hansen received a letter from the Danish Foreign Office informing him, 'the King, on representation of the Commercial Department dated 10th same month, had appointed Merchant Lorentz Hansen in Liverpool as Danish Consul...'.

However, his judgement of character proved not to be as successful as his work as the Danish Consul. Throughout the years 1805 to 1814 Hansen went through four partners and the firm, four changes of name. However, after Gerdes, Buschmann and Nicholls came the fourth partner, Charles Louis Bahr. Bahr proved to have more staying power than the previous partners but even so, the firm was not to remain Hansen and Bahr for very long. This time though, in 1816, it was Hansen himself that went, leaving Bahr total ownership of the firm which, by then, already handled work for ten ships.

Bahr went on to develop a highly successful shipbroking business dealing with upward of 500 ships annually. Indeed, Bahr's application for British nationality described him as running, 'one of the most extensive businesses as a Shipbroker in the kingdom' and in 1834, Bahr became one of the four original Liverpool subscribers to the reconstituted Lloyd's Register of Shipping. The firm remained C L Bahr until Bahr was joined by two Liverpool shipbrokers in 1835. The new partners were David Behrend and Henry Alexander Stewart and the firm became, Bahr, Behrend & Stewart.

Stewart retired in 1847 and died in the early 1850s. However, the partnership between Bahr and Behrend continued until it was broken by death. Bahr died in 1860 and Behrend died in 1863. Their sons, George Bahr and George Behrend took over the running of the business. It was the two George's that saw one of the most momentous years in the history of the firm. In 1852 the Serra Line was set up and throughout the whole second half of the 19th century enjoyed a major share of the trade between Liverpool and North and South Spain bringing the firm, who were shareholders in the Line, a prosperity and stability previously unmatched.

Left: *Lorenz Hansen.* **Right:** *The firm's business shown in the Liverpool Chronicle, 1828.* **Below:** *The firm's office on Chapel Street from 1899 to 1936, now the Liverpool Racquet Club.*

During the early 1860s, the firm needed an extra partner to take care of Black Sea Chartering. Consequently, A. Zeden was appointed but left in 1870 to set up his own Black Sea business in opposition to Bahr & Behrend. This opposition only lasted two years after which it failed and was dissolved.

By 1864, the firm, no longer desirous of trading as shipbrokers alone, described itself as 'Merchants, Shipbrokers and Steamship Agents'. The Merchants in the title referred to the firm's trade in cotton. However, the firm also had a regular Swedish trade and acted as Charterers of ships. In 1868 the firm moved from its premises in Cable Street to the greater comfort and increased prestige of the Old Castle Buildings in Preesons Row.

In 1880 George Bahr retired and in order to protect the Bahr interests in the firm until such time as his nephew could take his place, appointed Gordon Ross as partner. This proved to be an unpopular appointment and one which in the end almost brought the firm down. However, in the meantime the firm continued to flourish. In 1892, White Gann & Co, a Liverpool firm of shipowners with three steamers, came to grief. The Serra Company bought the steamers and gave them to Bahr Behrend & Ross to manage who accordingly opened a special Porto Rico department.

In 1894 the firm's fortunes started to turn. Against Gordon Ross' wishes, George Behrend's son, Harry, joined the firm. Gordon Ross was not happy and made it known that when the firm's contract with Serra came to an end in 1898, he intended to go off and take the Serra Line with him. Unfortunately, this is exactly what transpired but along with the Serra Line, Gordon also took the firm's Porto Rico steamers. The only thing stopping Gordon from taking the firm's name was a clause in the founding contract saying that in the event of a partnership breakdown, the Behrend's owned the name. This clause did, in fact, save the firm and although it was greatly reduced with only a Swedish Line and the shipbroking business left, new offices were found in Chapel Street and it managed to continue in business.

Fortunately, Gordon had brought with him some iron business in the shape of a Sicily sulphur mine, the Giona. The mine was thought to be nearly played out but after Gordon's departure, by some quirk of fate, it picked up again and over the following 20 years the firm received over £20,000 as its share of its output.

In 1904, Harry took over his father's share of the business and under his guidance, the firm began to work its way up again. Harry's brother George retired from the firm in this year but his other brother, Edward or Teddy as he was known, worked in the cash department before becoming a partner in

Below: One of Bahr Behrend's Liners being towed into deep water away from the port of Liverpool in the 1960s.

1906. The firm opened an office in Bradford to handle its textile business, in 1909 an office was opened in Manchester and in 1913, a further office was opened in London to develop opportunities for tobacco shipping.

This proved to be a far sighted move and the London office was later instrumental in attracting new Liner representations and Chartering links. During the first world war, 14 of the firm's staff volunteered for the army and although the firm remained in business it experienced a levelling off in its progress. It was not until after the war that the firm finally began to turn the corner. This was in part due to the sudden value attached to share certificates in Scandinavian steamers, of which the firm had many.

However, this success was also due to the fact that in 1921, after Harry's death, Arthur Behrend joined the firm and he, along with Harry's brother Teddy, ran the business. Activity increased further with the development of the Swedish trade (Swedish Lloyd) and the acquisition of a new Spanish Line, Anzar. In 1928 yet another office was opened, this time in Huddersfield. Unlike the firm's other successful offices, the Huddersfield one had to be closed down two years later because it was not making any money. This was followed with a more positive move in 1936 when the firm's Liverpool office was moved from Chapel Street to India Buildings.

The advent of the second world war brought about several changes for the firm. Fortunately, in the 1930s Bahr Behrend had acquired a major sheet metal manufacturer, John Summers & Sons as a client. This connection, coupled with the firm's traditional involvement with the tobacco industry, enabled it to make a significant contribution to the war effort. Indeed, the war quickly diverted the tobacco trade of Britain into fresh channels. Shortage of ships and dollars swept away the existing order of tobacco buying, and bombing brought about innovative new methods of tobacco storage. During this time Bahr Behrend played a major part in ensuring Churchill's demand that troops and factory workers should have their cigarettes. A few months after completing this task, due to the work of Thomas Meadway augmented in London by Peat and Davey, the firm was appointed agents for the Board of Trade to cover clearance at all English ports apart from London of American lease-lend tobacco in hogsheads. However, it was

*Top: A modern container vessel. **Above:** Staff in Head Office in the mid 1990s.*

also in 1941 that the firm's offices at India Buildings were bombed and went up in flames taking the firm's stock of 2000 cigars with it! The company then moved temporarily to offices in Old Hall Street, to return in 1951 to a restored India Buildings.

The shipping trade was also a changed one after the war and Bahr Behrend took advantage of this, taking on agency work for new shipping lines, some of which still feature amongst the company's liner agency activities. In 1958 the firm had grown to such an extent that it was able to be incorporated as a private Limited Company and over the following years continued to thrive under this new status.

In 1989, as the fifth generation of the Behrend family reached retirement, the majority of the company shares were transferred to an Employee Benefit Trust in order to safeguard the company's independent status. Indeed, this status remained and by 1998, the company's Liner Agency business had developed and expanded to such an extent that a separate company, Bahr Behrend Agencies Limited, was formed to concentrate solely on this side of the business.

Today the Bahr Behrend Group comprises five companies with Bahr Behrend & Co. Ltd as the Holding Company: Bahr Behrend Agencies Ltd (Liner Agency), Bahr Forwarding Ltd (International Freight Forwarding), Bornholm Transport Ltd (Transport and Haulage services) and Bahr Projects Ltd (Project Forwarding).

New international names have also been added to the company's long standing list of clients and the company's activities are accredited to BS EN ISO 9002 Quality Assurance. Bahr Behrend's headquarters remain in Liverpool and the company now has extra operational offices in Felixstowe, London, Sheffield, Bradford and Birmingham with over 125 staff. Indeed, most of today's business systems would have been unrecognisable to Bahr Behrend's founding fathers of the 18th Century but the basic principles which underlined their business approach - professionalism and integrity - remain the hallmarks of the company today and it is this that will ensure that Bahr Behrend stays afloat for many more years to come.

Top: A Bornholm Transport vehicle at the Pier Head.
Above left: *The Bi-Centenary celebration Luncheon in 1993.* ***Below:*** *The current Main Board of Directors.*

Standard bearers flying the flag in Liverpool

Porter's of Liverpool was originally set up during the years before the advent of the first world war by Herbert Gordon Porter. Before setting up his own business the firm's founder was gathering experience working for the shipping merchants in Liverpool. Throughout his work, the enterprising Herbert noticed that the shipping merchants were always being asked for flags. At that time, there were no flag makers in the city and the merchants found it very difficult to meet their customer's demands. Herbert saw a gap in the market and after a falling out with his employers, he summoned up all his entrepreneurial spirit and decided to fill this gap by setting up a flag making business of his own.

Herbert launched his fledgling venture on the Dock Road in Liverpool and employed a couple of machinists to help with the production of the flags. Indeed, he must have been a good and fair employer as the machinists actually worked at Porter's for over 50 years! In the early days of the business the flags were sold to the shipping companies in the thriving port of Liverpool. However, this work was complemented with the addition of another side of the business run by Herbert's brother Harry who was in charge of supplying cleaning and wiping rags to the ships' merchants.

By the 1920s the business had developed to such an extent that it was necessary to move to new premises located further along the Old Dock Road. From there, as well as the production of flags, cotton waste was

Right: *Staff hard at work during the 1950s.*
Below: *Delivery trucks outside the firm's premises in 1954.*

delivered for engine cleaning; rags and offcuts bought from the Lancashire factories were cleaned using the laundry down the road. This success was compounded in 1921 when Porter's of Liverpool became a Limited Company.

By the 1930s Porter's employed approximately 20 to 30 staff and with their help, the use of agents across the world and the Crown Agents in London, began to build up what was to become a valuable export business supplying governments across the world.

The advent of the second world war brought with it temporary changes to the running of the company. Porter's was, in fact, making Nazi flags for the Germans and the onset of war saw this order being cancelled. Despite this, work was far from sparse. Indeed, throughout the hostilities Porter's conducted a lot of work for the MoD and even made flags for the D-day landings.

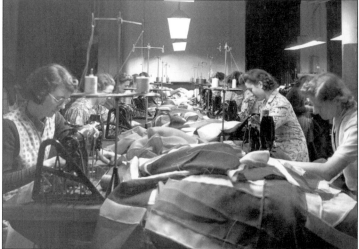

The post-war years continued to be productive ones for the company and by the 1950s Porter's had developed even further and employed a total of 70 to 80 people. Herbert had accomplished his goal of filling the gap in the market and building up a successful flag making business. Indeed, when he took semi-retirement during the 1960s Herbert passed a flourishing concern on to his son, Robert Gordon Porter who took over the running of the family firm.

Sadly, in 1973, after continuing his involvement in the company throughout his retirement, the founder died. However, under his son's leadership, Porter's of Liverpool continued to thrive. The company progressed throughout

the following decades and managed to adapt to changes and advancements in the trade. Although Porter's maintained the tradition of making its high quality flags by hand, modern printing methods were taken on and currently digital printing is available if required.

In 1994, Robert Porter took semi-retirement. However, to this day he still works at the company for two days a week. Robert's son, Michael Gordon Porter took over the running of the firm and is still Porter's managing director today.

Over its history Porter's of Liverpool has supplied its products to several famous and distinguished customers for important events. Porter's made the coffin drape for Churchill's funeral and supplied flags for the Silver Jubilee and the Coronation. The firm also made the curtains for the entrance of the opening of the Mersey Tunnel in 1934. However, three days before the opening ceremony it was decided that the curtains were too plain and consequently, Porter's staff worked through the night for two days adding Liver Birds to them! In 1982 Ranulph Fiennes came to Porter's to purchase a flag for his expedition to the North Pole and in 1986 an RAF pilot aboard the Space Shuttle Challenger carried a Porter's flag. However, most notably, in 1999 an historic Porter's flag used by Robert Scott in 1912 to plunge into the ice of the South Pole was sold at auction for £25,300.

Today, Porter's of Liverpool employ over 50 people and many of its flags are manufactured for the British armed forces and for advertising purposes. The company also supplies high quality cleaning cloths for Rolls Royce and a large range of packaging materials. After over 90 years in business Porter's really is a standard-bearer, flying the flag of success in Liverpool.

Top: *The pattern cutting room in the 1950s.*
Above left: *Porter Bros. flags in 1957.*

Silverbeck Rymer - A firm commitment to practising excellence

The Liverpool based leading firm of Solicitors, Silverbeck Rymer was originally established in 1946 by Nathan Silverbeck. The firm's founder had served in the second world war as a Wing Commander in charge of Biggin Hill, the airfield famed for the exploits of its pilots in the Battle of Britain. It was after his demobilisation from the Royal Airforce at the cessation of hostilities that Nathan made the enterprising decision to set up a practice of his own.

The fledgling firm began from premises located above Rigby's pub in Dale Street, Liverpool and in these early years, set up as a general legal practice with a strong bias towards domestic conveyancing.

It was not long before Nathan's firm began to flourish and in 1949 he was able to incorporate another solicitor into his practice. After completing his wartime service in the Intelligence Corps in Egypt, Palestine and Syria, Sidney Brayde joined the practice which, at that time, had one legal desk and two typists. Most of the work carried out by the firm was still in the domestic and commercial property fields. However, a small amount was matrimonial, criminal, insurance and general work. In one memorable case the firm was instructed to act

for a Polish man who was accused of a particularly gruesome murder. He was eventually found to be guilty but due to the efforts of the firm, not insane.

In 1959 the firm added another partner to its repertoire in the shape of Bernard Wolfson (who subsequently became District Judge Wolfson). With his help, the practice began to attract a larger and heavier volume of defendant insurance and other litigation work. This change in focus was accomplished in order to make up for the less and less remunerative domestic and conveyance scene. The change in direction was forged with the first restructure in the firm's history. Nathan took on the role of Managing Director, Sidney acted as Head of the Property and Commercial Department and Bernard became the Head of the Insurance and Litigation Department.

In 1978 Nathan Silverbeck retired from the practice. Under this newly organised structure the firm continued to thrive and the litigation department continued to grow. In 1979, to cope with the increased workload, the firm took on another partner, Jim Rymer.

Below: *The firm's Brunswick Street premises.*

Jim had originally joined the practice as a Junior Clerk and after qualifying was sent to take charge of the newly opened branch in Bootle. It was from Bootle that Jim began to follow his own particular legal star by displaying his expertise and enthusiasm in Civil Litigation. Indeed, the development of the Bootle office played a significant role in the firm's development.

As well as the Bootle branch the firm had also acquired an established practice in Kirkby and this was followed with the opening of two further branches in Litherland and Huyton. Despite these ever increasing developments it was not until the mid 1980s that the firm began its period of rapid and tremendous growth.

From the mid 1980s the firm's focus turned to the development of the commercial business. The expansion of work in the Liverpool office led to the practice centralising its operations in the city centre and basing its headquarters in Liverpool.

By 1993 the firm had outgrown its Liverpool city centre offices and so, after a refurbishment to provide a modern office, the practice moved to its current location, the Grade II Listed Heywoods Building in Brunswick Street. Once settled in the new premises, the firm developed two separate departments for the Claimant and Defendant client bases which, as well as coping with the rising workloads, gave greater specialisation to the practice. Indeed, one of the firm's partners, Patricia Ewen became a director and the head of the newly separated Plaintiff (now Claimant) Litigation Department.

From the mid 1980s the firm's focus turned to the development of the commercial business

The litigation work increased and in 1997, Silverbeck Rymer opened a second office in Chelmsford to look after the southern and London work which assisted the rapid growth in the financial turnover. This office was opened under the management of partner Charles Rymer. This was followed with the opening of a third office after the acquisition of the lions share of business and client portfolios and significant partner acquisitions from Manchester firm, Geoffrey Warhurst and Co in the year 2000. Three of the Manchester firm's partners, Keith Popperwell, Nick Goddard and Phil D'Netto joined Silverbeck Rymer after the take-over. The two firms had much in common, both working for the Insurance Industry and thus, the merger was successful.

Today, assisted by the Warhurst acquisitions, the firm continues to thrive, ever expanding its litigation work and strong links with the insurance industry. Silverbeck Rymer has captured a large market share of business from the UKs major insurance companies; has a large claimant litigations department dealing with both motor and non-motor claims, contractual disputes, debt recovery, and actions in tort; and a rapidly growing technical injury department. Indeed, with its firm commitment to practising excellence and exceeding clients' expectations, Silverbeck Rymer is set to continue its rapid growth into the future.

Above: *Top left: Jim Rymer, Senior Partner from 1984 to date.* **Top right:** *Sidney Brayde.*

A source of quality for over 60 years

The Liverpool sales and marketing company Lawtons was established in 1935 under the name, Lawtons Supply Company. Its founding fathers were two brothers, Arnold and Fred Stevens who between them, named their fledgling firm after the site of its first premises in Lawton Road, Crosby. The company was originally founded in order to sell office stationery. However, by 1946 the firm's range had extended to include industrial staplers.

It was not long before Lawtons Supply Company began to thrive and as the business grew, larger premises were required. Consequently, in 1940 the business moved to new premises located at 14 Cable Street. This move was followed in 1946 by two more consecutive moves to yet larger and further improved premises. The first one was situated at 80 Whitechapel and the second at 46 Park Lane.

By 1960 Lawtons had become the best known wholesaler of stationery in the North West of England and required even bigger premises. This time the company decided not to take any chances and consequently, purchased purpose built premises located at LAWCO House, Vauxhall Road. Originally these premises consisted of three floors and as such, provided sufficient space for the new products that had been added to the company's existing range. These included new coding and marking products and a range of steel and plastic strapping tools and consumables.

In 1964 two additional floors were added to the building in order to accommodate the new manual range of fresh produce, pre-packing tools and consumables which had also been added to the Lawtons portfolio of products.

As an extremely successful office products business, Lawtons proved to be a very attractive proposition. Indeed, Ofrex plc, who owned the Rexel brand of office stapling products, found this to be so and in 1965 acquired Lawtons. In turn, Ofrex itself was acquired in 1975 by American Brands who went on to direct Ofrex to concentrate on its core activity as a manufacturer. This led to conflict for Ofrex as, in direct competition to it, Lawtons were selling office stationery products. Therefore, in order to avoid this conflict, Lawtons phased out its trading of general stationery products and began concentrating on industrial products. In return, the Ofrex Group delegated the responsibility of one of its subsidiary companies, British Industrial Fastening to Lawtons who took over the concern.

By 1980, the coding and marking business had begun to be established. Lawtons itself, played a major role in the pioneering of the introduction of the concept of continuous small character and dot-on-demand large character coding into the United Kingdom.

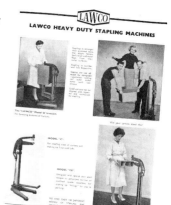

The storage needs of the industrial product range was significantly different to that of the general stationery. Therefore, in order to store and distribute the product range the Ellesmere Port distribution centre was acquired in 1987. Located on the Rossmore industrial estate the site consists of a 32,000 sq. ft. warehouse plus additional office space.

In 1992 the Ofrex Group decided to concentrate once again on its core business of office products. Lawtons' product range no longer fitted this description and as a

Top right: *A page from a 1950s product brochure.* ***Right:*** *The interior of one of the warehouses, in the 1970s.*

result, because the company was felt to be surplus to Ofrex's strategy, the Group looked to sell it. Fortunately, the management of Lawtons was allowed to bid and in fact, was successful with an M.B.O. and on the 14th of July, 1992 acquired the company. After the buyout, major investment took place in the company with particular emphasis placed on areas which would significantly improve service and response times to the customer base.

To this day, Lawtons continues to trade from Lawco House, Liverpool and despatches products from its distribution centre nationally across the UK as well as to a number of countries overseas. In 1999 Lawtons Vauxhall Road offices underwent a vast renovation programme involving both structural and cosmetic changes. These changes resulted in, from the outside, an obviously more modern looking building but most importantly, on the inside, a better and more professional business environment benefiting both employees and customers alike.

Lawtons has a separate warehousing and distribution centre in order to facilitate the stock and response levels required from the huge and varied customer base it services. As an international sales and marketing company Lawtons is involved in the source and supply of flooring products, packaging machines and consumables, fresh produce packing equipment, specialist storage and filing, and engineering support services. Overall, Lawtons employs approximately 100 people who, together with its trading name, reputation, and quality of products, are the main assets of the business that will ensure its success for the next 60 years - at least!

Top: Head office in the 1970s. **Above left:** *The newly refurbished Head office.* **Below:** *The Management Team from left to right: K Mohan, Technical Director; D Mohan, Financial Director; D A Hughes, Managing Director; J E Reid, Sales and Marketing Director.*

T&J Harrison - Liverpool shipowners since the 1830s

The history of Harrison Line, managed by Thos. & Jas. Harrison Ltd., within the Charente Group of Companies, can be traced back as far as 1830. It was in that year that the Company's founder, Thomas Harrison, first became involved in ship-owning and agency work. This came about when he started working for the Firm of Samuel Brown and Son and Co.

This Firm operated from King Street in Liverpool, as an agent for shippers, charterers and ship-owners. During his time with the Company, Thomas gathered experience that was later to prove invaluable and gradually he acquired shares in the Firm and in the ships that they operated. Eight years later, Thomas was joined by his brother, James Harrison, and it was not long after this that their brothers John and Edward Harrison became involved as shareholders also.

The year 1853 was a notable one in the history of the Company, for it was in that year that the last of the Brown family died and Thomas and James Harrison formed a Partnership. The style of the business was therefore changed to Thomas and James Harrison.

At this stage of the Firm's development the main activity of the newly named company was that of operating sailing ships trading from Britain to France with coal and returning with brandies. These were imported from the Bordeaux area, centred on the town of Cognac and the Charente river valley, with Tonnay-Charente as the loading port. Although this made up the main part of the Company's activities, other vessels, either wholly or part owned, ventured further afield, in fact

Above: Thomas Harrison (square picture), James Harrison (round picture). Right: Edward Harrison (larger picture), John Harrison (smaller picture). Below: The Canada Dock in August 1966, with the Harrison ships MV FACTOR, MV DISCOVERER, MV GOVERNOR, MV CUSTODIAN and SS FORESTER alongside.

to most parts of the world. Amongst these vessels was the ship rigged PHILOSOPHER of 1857, Harrisons first iron hull and the first to be named after a trade or profession - a tradition that continues to this day and by which the Company's vessels are readily recognised.

Harrison Line developed and grew into an ever more successful and flourishing concern and by 1884, as sail was giving way to steam, the Partnership owned a fleet of 22 vessels. In that year the Charente Steam-Ship Company was officially formed, to take over the ownership of the ships and other assets. Thos. & Jas. Harrison was appointed Manager of the holding company's fleet and operations.

Under this new management structure, Harrison Line continued to maintain its outstanding position in the market place, enabling it to develop successfully into the following century. Subsequently however, two world wars brought upheaval and during these hostilities, the Firm lost a total of 53 ships and with them, devastatingly, 536 Harrison seafarers perished.

One incident from World War II, that eventually became folklore, concerned the Harrison vessel POLITICIAN. In 1941 she ran aground in bad weather and was wrecked on the Scottish Isle of Eriskay. In a happy coincidence for the local inhabitants, she was carrying a cargo that included 275,000 bottles of whisky. This incident became widely known and was the inspiration for the book and subsequent classic comedy film 'Whisky Galore'. (In Compton Mackenzie's tale the ship was called CABINET MINISTER).

By the middle of the last century the Firm's interests had expanded to include Liner trading with the Caribbean and Latin America and South and East Africa. In 1950, Thos. & Jas. Harrison became a limited liability Company.

In the 1970s the Company decided to diversify and invested in dry bulk carriers which traded world wide and in 1977, their first container ships were built for the newly containerised Caribbean trade.

Harrisons have always maintained a friendly, courteous approach to their customers, with personal service and attention to detail. In 1987, this was recognised when the Company received one of the first awards inaugurated by the Shipping Press. Remarkably Harrison Line has continued to receive awards in every subsequent year when presentations have taken place.

In 1994 this success was reinforced when the Company's head office in Liverpool obtained its initial Quality Management Certificate (Now BS EN ISO 9002). Three years later the Marine and Engineers Department, responsible for ship management, obtained its International Safety Management (ISM) compliance document and a joint venture company, named Bibby-Harrison Management Services, was successfully established with Bibby Line to manage the two Companies fleets and vessels belonging to third parties. The Charente Group also took an interest in LPG and Chemical tankers.

Above: *The ship WEST DERBY, in the company's fleet between 1855 and 1876, in the Mersey off Egremont.*

chart distributors - the latter also manufactures nautical instruments) the aforementioned Bibby-Harrison Management Services and S.C. Chambers (Britain's largest ship sale and purchase Brokers outside London).

As an independent private Firm with over a century and a half of experience, Charente and Harrisons of Liverpool continues to remain equipped to compete effectively in today's world of multi-trade international operators.

Above left: *The SS POLITICIAN which was wrecked in 1941 with its cargo of whisky.*
Top: *The SS JARNAC c1910 at Tonnay-Charente.*
Below: *The company's head office, Mersey Chambers, overlooking St Nicholas' Churchyard and the River Mersey.*

Since 1998, the Company has been expanding in pursuance of its commitment to customer service, by diversifying into other transport related activities. The Tyrer and Bencher groups, both long established in transport logistics areas, were acquired and by the year 2000, the time had come to operate these under one brand name; Harrison Logistics Limited was formed to develop groupage, consolidation, clearing and forwarding, warehousing, distribution, European trailer and NVOC services, offered from offices throughout the United Kingdom, the Irish Republic and Holland.

Today, although Harrison Line and Harrison Logistics are both part of the Charente Group, they trade independently and the Line continues with its traditional shipowning and operating activities. Other member companies with the Group include Prentice, Service & Henderson (ships agents in Scotland), Dubois Phillips & McCallum and Lilley & Gillie (together the world's second largest Admiralty

Rising like a Phoenix from Liverpool's industrial heritage

Fire was the reason the Royal Insurance Company was founded. Liverpool's docks and warehouses were considered to be more vulnerable to fire than others in industrial Britain. The higher risk meant that the London insurance companies wanted to charge a higher premium for any Liverpool company wanting to insure against fire damage.

After the 'Formby Street Area' fire of 1842, valuable buildings were lost at a cost of £1 million (£150 million today) causing the London insurance companies to raise their premiums. Liverpool merchants were outraged and on 11 March 1845 a group of prominent merchants and businessmen formed a 'Joint Stock Fire and Life Insurance Association' named Royal.

The first 50 years
The second half of the nineteenth century saw Liverpool challenging London for the status of Britain's premier port. The Royal took full advantage of Liverpool's growing prosperity and made a profit in each of its first ten years.

A turning point for the Royal came in 1888, when the income from fire premiums exceeded £1 million, 'the first time that any fire insurance company has ever obtained £1,000,000 sterling from fire revenue without having amalgamated with some company'.

By the end of its first 50 years the Royal was the largest fire insurer in the world and contributed to extending the influence of British insurance across the globe.

The second 50 years
Over the next 50 years or so the company's claim-paying reputation resulted in increased levels of new business. Despite difficult financial years in the 1920s, the Royal maintained an even keel and was even able to weather the Great Depression of the early 1930s.

The Royal came out of the second world war in a healthy position with new record premiums of £17.6 million for its fire, accident and marine lines and a steady set of trading results for its overseas business.

The increasing prosperity of the 1950s and 1960s was matched by an expansion of the insurance business to cover all of the public's new material possessions. Difficulty in profiting

from motor insurance business led to spectacular company collapses in the late 1960s and early 1970s and the spiralling inflation of the 1960s turned the Royal's £12.4 million UK underwriting profit of 1972 into a £5.1 million loss in 1973.

The Royal benefited from the recession of the early 1980s, with high interest rates bringing higher investment income and a falling pound boosting overseas earnings.

The recent years
In February 1992 the board took the plunge and omitted its final dividend after announcing losses of £373 million for 1991 - double those of the previous year.

The Royal was battered on all fronts - by recession, low share prices, bitter price competition, domestic mortgage indemnity losses and losses through the estate agency operation. It was evident that recovery in the low inflation environment of the 1990s could only be sustained by sensible, selective underwriting, since return on investments would be lower and could no longer be counted on to cancel out underwriting losses.

The Royal merged with Sun Alliance in 1996 to form Royal & SunAlliance. Today, Royal & SunAlliance manage total investments of over £57 billion for over 4 million customers.

The company still has roots in Liverpool, with its UK Head Office housing 3,500 employees. From its humble beginnings, Royal & SunAlliance now has a truly global presence, operating in 55 countries.

Above: *The Royal's fire mark - which would identify a building insured by the company and ensure that any fire would be extinguished by the Royal's own fire brigade.* ***Below:*** *The Royal & SunAlliance's new building in Liverpool, one of the largest office blocks in Europe.*

The legacy of Liverpool's caring father

In St John's Gardens, Liverpool, there stands a memorial statue to Fr Nugent, erected by public subscription after his death. During his lifetime Fr Nugent had worked tirelessly to improve life for Liverpool's underprivileged classes, and as a result of his efforts a great deal had been done to help the homeless and poverty-stricken children of the district. But perhaps more important still is the legacy which he left to carry on his good work: The Nugent Care Society.

Although society has changed a good deal in the last hundred years, the basic need for a caring, supportive environment where youngsters can learn and grow up, and for suitable living accommodation for people of every age, remain as important today as ever. However, it was the plight of the children which shocked Liverpool-born James Nugent when, having trained for the priesthood, he came back to his native city as curate at St Nicholas' Pro-cathedral, Copperas Hill - the church where he had been baptised. Living conditions around the docks where the immigrant workers lived were so bad that epidemics were rife; hundreds of people died of typhoid and cholera, and as a result many penniless orphans were left to try and scrape together a living on the streets. Ragged Schools existed, and provided the children with food and shelter during the day, but these, together with the prison and the workhouse, represented the extent of the assistance which the city offered its orphans. Fr Nugent made it his mission to attack this problem, and he did this in a number of ways: by raising public awareness and instituting a Children's Charter which was signed by the leading churchmen of all persuasions; by opening a Night Refuge at 22 and 24 Soho Street in 1864; and by setting up two Catholic Schools, which were followed by orphanages, reformatories, mother and baby homes, hostels for single men and women and training schools including HMS Clarence which, for many years, was moored in The Sloyne channel off New Ferry. He was also active in securing good homes in Canada and the United States for the large numbers of children who were sent to those countries under the mass emigration programmes organised by the Government, the Trade Unions and the Church.

Above: The statue of Monsignor Nugent St. John's Gardens, unveiled in December 1906. **Below:** *HMS Clarence trained lads to serve in the Merchant Navy.*

Disadvantaged members of the community can obtain information and advice on matters such as health, education, benefits, employment, and fuel, as well as material assistance in the form of clothing and household items, from the Community Resource service. The Society also offers short or long-term residential care at Residential and Nursing Homes throughout the area, both for older people and for adults whose mental or physical health makes it impractical for them to live independently. A range of support services and counselling is offered for various groups including deaf people and people with a learning disability who do live independently within the community but who stand to benefit from special care. And of course, true to the spirit of Fr Nugent, a great deal is done for the area's children. The Society runs three community homes for children up to the age of 18; Clumber Lodge, Othona and St Catherine's Centre for Girls which has both secure and open units and facilities for independence training. It also manages a children's home owned by the Sisters of Nazareth. In addition, the Society provides education for children with social, emotional or behavioural difficulties, and is a registered Adoption Agency. The work which was begun by one man has grown into the country's biggest regional care society, employing around 800 people and improving the lives of countless adults and children in Liverpool today.

Fr Nugent died in 1903 at the age of 81, having succeeded in bringing about tremendous improvements to the social conditions in Liverpool. Contemporary reports show that he remained to the end of his days a charismatic man and an eloquent speaker with the power to communicate his own enthusiasm to his audience. He would have been gratified to see the extent to which his efforts inspired his successors to carry on his work with the city's poor, and he would certainly approve of the work of The Nugent Care Society today.

***Above left:** Just visible behind Kelton Grange, one of the most modern of the Society's homes, is part of the 'House of Providence', a mother and baby home founded by Fr Nugent. It was later enlarged by the addition of the Victorian Gothic building on the left and was renamed 'Kelton'. The original buildings now house the Staff Training Centre. **Top left:** The Society's Court Missionary visiting a family in Bevington Bush in the 1960s.*

A reputation of over 130 years standing

The architect, surveyor and property consultant organisation, Edmund Kirby and Sons was founded in the 1860s by Edmund Kirby. Before setting up in practice as an architect, Edmund had studied at the Royal Academy School of Art. He was then articled to the architect Edward Welby Pugin and later worked for ecclesiastical designer, Hardman & Co followed by the Chester architect, John Douglas.

It is not known exactly when Edmund set up his own practice. However, in 1868 he was operating from offices located at Derby Buildings in Fenwick Street, Liverpool. Soon, Edmund had built up a first rate practice and by 1878 he was able to move to new offices in Union Buildings, Cook Street, completed to his own design.

In 1888 Edmund was elected FRIBA, a Fellow of the Surveyors Institution and a Surveyor to the Board of Trade. By 1899 Edmund had taken on assistants. Arthur Oswald Power was articled to the firm and the names, Moller, Chopping and Smout appeared as assistants. However, it was not until 1901 that the practice became a family concern. Edmund's son, Edmund Bertram Kirby (Bertie), joined the practice after training as an architect and was followed by his eldest brother, Francis J Kirby, in 1905 who joined as a surveyor and was proud to be a member of the Surveyor's Institution. It was in 1905 that the practice became known as Edmund Kirby & Sons.

Before the advent of the first world war, Edmund had been the President of Liverpool Architectural Society. Bertie went to war whilst Francis stayed to run the firm. After the war, Francis was appointed to the Mersey Tunnel Joint Committee and Bertie continued in the architectural practice which culminated in the design of the Women's Hospital opened by the Duchess of York (now the Queen Mother).

Sadly, in 1920 Edmund Kirby died. He left a legacy of commissions including the design of 14 churches for the diocese of Shrewsbury alone, 15 Roman Catholic Schools, hospitals, workhouse buildings and private and commercial properties.

By the advent of the second world war, Douglas Pitts and then Peter Rowland had become successive partners. They and Bertie held the firm together during the war when most of the staff were at war. After the war, Bertie retired, the practice underwent a modernisation to departmentalise skills and much work was carried out requisitioning properties and repairing bomb damage.

In 1954 a pilot firm, EJ Battersby and Frith was launched in Wigan but after a successful period was amalgamated with the practice in 1966. In the previous year the practice had moved to State House, built to the firm's design and Douglas retired, though sadly Peter had died in 1964. However, by its centenary in 1968 the firm was thriving and continued to complete successful commissions.

The practice moved to India Buildings in 1986 and it is from there that Edmund Kirby continues to function. Today, Douglas' son Michael is amongst the eight partners and although the firm now has the added facet of being a property consultancy, it still draws on experience built up over more than 130 years of successful business.

Above left: Edmund Kirby, who founded the company in the 1860s. **Right:** *Liverpool's Passport office, designed by the company.* **Below:** *Water Street, Liverpool.*

Following that dream

The Liverpool company, Rewinds & J Windsor and Sons (Engineers) Ltd was founded in 1946 by John I Windsor.

At the close of the second world war, John I Windsor set up a business on his own after gaining experience as an engineer. However, his ambitious and entrepreneurial spirit now led him to a new area of expertise. John recognised that there was a gap in the market and promptly founded his own business to fill it.

Early days
Consequently, John's new firm, set up to repair and sell vacuum cleaners, began trading in Wood Street in Liverpool under the name Rewinds and proved to be a success. Indeed, only two years after its foundation, in 1948, the firm expanded, in a natural progression of development, to include the repair of electric motors with a specialisation in marine work.

In the 1950s Michael Windsor, eldest son of John I Windsor, joined as a Chartered Engineer after gaining marine experience at sea. The following decade saw John, Michael's younger brother, join the business and further factories were opened on the Poulton Industrial Estate and the present main factory on Regent Road, Liverpool.

Recent changes
The 1980s were important years for the business. During this time another generation of Windsor's, Luke, Ruth, Lee and Scott, joined the family firm. Also, a GEC Licence was acquired and the company began its export business selling motors to India, the USA, South Africa and the Philippines.

During the 1990s, the success of the firm continued despite the sad departure of its founder who died in 1991. Two additional factories were purchased in Worsley, Manchester and in Bolton. This brings the group's employment level to over 150 people.

Today, Rewinds & J Windsor and Sons (Engineers) Ltd remains a family run engineering company carrying out electric motor rewinds as well as providing general machining and dynamic balancing services. With a fast changing world, the electronic section, a recent development, is meeting today's requirements for high tech services of electronic repair and installation.

Below: *John I Windsor, second from right, who founded the company at the end of the second world war, and his eldest son Michael. They are pictured next to a balancing machine manufactured by the company in 1968, for export to South Korea.*

The Liverpool waterfront has changed out of all recognition since 1930, when this scene was pictured, but the city's ambitious regeneration schemes have recently given the area a new lease of life.

Acknowledgments

The publishers would like to thank

Liverpool Libraries and Information Services

Oxton Studios

Freddy O'Connor who edited the book

Everton Football Club

Members of the Liverpool and South West Lancashire Family History Society

Thanks are also due to Peggy Burns who penned the editorial text

and Ann Ramsdale for her copywriting skills